Before and After Your Big

PAYDAY!

Your business SOLD,
Congratulations. You Earned It.

NOW WHAT?
How to Prepare for and Protect your
Sudden Wealth™
Before and after you sell your company
and how to keep it

By Two Time National Best Selling Author
Mitchell Levin, MD, CWPP, CAPP
The Financial Physician™

FIRST EDITION

ISBN: 978-0-9907906-2-4

Other books by Dr. Mitchell Levin

How Elite Advisors GROW!

Power Principles for Success

Goal! The Financial Physician's Ultimate Survival Guide for the Professional Athlete

Shift Happens

Smart Choices for Serious Money

Cover Your Assets: How to Build, Protect and Maintain Your Own Financial Fortress

Table of Contents

Disclosures and disclaimers:
This book is not giving legal or tax advice. Investments involve risk of loss. Insurance and annuity products depend on the claims paying abilities of the carriers.

This book will not be a re-hash of my other books. Though it contains many of the principles that are the core of the strategies revealed here. Instead, this book compiles the necessary facts, and strategies you and business owners need to know to optimize your business' value.

Acknowledgments:
Many thanks to Nick Rodites for inspiration and critique; to ACG for the reason; to Paul Stefan for encouragement; to Ray Watson for believing; to Brett Fadely for validating.

I would also like to thank John LaLonde, Ted Oakley, Roccy DeFrancesco, The Wealth Preservation Institute, Don Blanton, MoneyTrax, Kevin Fink, Dan Kennedy, Ken Crabtree, Chris Music, Nick Nanton, Jack Dicks, Matt Zagula, Mike Rossi, Jason Graham, Association for Corporate Growth, and so many more who have embraced or discussed elsewhere the subjects I have described for this book.

Feel free to share this with those who may be recipients of Sudden Wealth™. Feel free also to share this book with the attorneys, accountants, business brokers, investment bankers, and other professionals who assist clients of Sudden Wealth™, too.

Introduction

Exit, Stage Left?

The exit plan, for many business owners, *if we even have one* -- is to sell our business...someday, to someone. Our business is more than our source of income, it is our retirement plan. Often it is our legacy plan, too; and to some even our identity.

What if we do sell? To whom? How do we handle that Sudden Wealth™? What are the benefits, the risks, the alternatives, and the likely outcomes of selling? After we *monetize*, and exit the business, now what?

What if we cannot or should not sell our business? Can we monetize our business another way? How? These are questions many have in the back of our minds.

Billy sold his manufacturing business for $50 million 25 years ago. Now, he recently was forced to sell his *mansion* to preserve some lifestyle.

Annie received $2 million in cash for her marketing business, plus a $2Million note at 10% for 3 years. A few short years later, she ran out of money.

John's food service and distribution $23 Million annual sales business sold for $14 million. It consisted of $8 Million in cash plus a 5 year "earn out" if certain hurdles were met. One year and 9 months later, he is in litigation with the buyer, has not received one dollar of the earn-out, his cash is down to $5.6 Million, and he faces over $200,000 in legal fees. Not only that, John's buyer has decimated the business, the key employees have left, John is 72, and he no longer has the fire in the belly to help rebuild should he be successful in regaining control as a result of the litigation.

Ken's multi-chain restaurant franchise business did over $150 Million in sales. He sold to a *strategic* buyer for $130 Million in cash. Three years later, he was diagnosed with ALS, a debilitating nerve disease that eventually will leave him physically incapable. His children are spending their inheritance, and thwarting his attempts to set up a foundation for ALS research. In one more generation, there may be no more funds.

Jack ran his business for 30 years. He started the business with less than $3000, now it has sales over $20 million. He took out what he needed, when he needed it. He re-invested all the rest back into the business. When Jack tried to sell, he had few offers. None satisfactory. His business had little value to a buyer because he had no plan in place for the exit. The business was completely dependent upon him to generate new sales and to deliver the "product". Jack himself would not pay to buy his business what his offering price was.

Billy is an Ivy League educated, very successful businessman. Annie had the misfortune of not understanding her lifestyle needs. John had studiously and diligently plowed *all* his profits back into the business. Ken's cash went into funding "businesses' for his children, Jack's business is an ill-liquid, micro-cap stock, with high risk, and Jack was not diversified. All share similar unhappy, unfortunate, and completely avoidable outcomes.

Your business is an asset worth money. It will not sell itself. Is it even salable? Could your business get passed over due to risk?

38% expect a big check, according to the National Association of Independent Business Owners.

Too many owners have no idea what their business is worth, at what price, and on what terms.

Too many often put more thought into stocks they buy and sell than their own business. Who are the buyers?

No other book has addressed these issues.

Does any of this sound familiar? Are you thinking this cannot happen to me, or this is not me? Is there a little "*shadenfreude*," the German phrase for joy at someone else's suffering? Is there a wonder if this could happen to you? Or even how could his possible happen?

In these pages, we will show you why and how it happens. Most importantly, we will show you how to avoid it, and how to make your business do exactly what you intend upon your exit.

You may sneer at the athlete (see my book, "***GOAL the Ultimate Survival Guide for the Professional Athlete***"), or someone who was a lottery winner, and eventually goes broke. Maybe they were imprudent or uneducated, or maybe not. We are talking in these pages about good people who deserve better than they are otherwise receiving.

We will explore the Sudden Wealth™ and the different types of people. We will also touch on how to help you attain and retain your newly found liquidity. And, we will discuss the systemic flaws that we overcome in helping clients preserve, protect and prosper from Sudden Wealth™.

We hope you enjoy this book. It is not necessary to read in its entirety. Rather, first look at the myths and the realities. Then look at the chapters that may help you to help others. This book is organized into four phases: 1) prior to the sale 2) preparing for the sale 3) methods of monetizing, and 4) the post-close.

Most importantly, thank you for helping us improve the world, one client at a time. As they say in Australia, "good on ya', mate!"

Section One
Prior to and Preparing for the Sale

Chapter 1
"Pursuit of Happiness"

Those words are an absolute game changer. Before those words, everybody was doing something for the benefit of the state, the king, the church, whomever. Now we had the right to enjoy what we produced. Not the right to enjoy what someone else had produced for us, but the right to enjoy what we produced.

Why not pursue the happiness, enjoy the right of what you've built, what you've produced?

Too many of us business owners focus on the top line. When you have that top line focus, you are certainly growing in revenues. And where do most of those revenues go? They go to taxes. They go to regulation compliance. They go to your landlord. They go to your finance companies. They go to your suppliers. They go to your employees. And then finally you can get paid.

And how many times have we seen that the pay the owner gets from his business is far below what someone would have to pay if we had to replace the owner if we owned the business. Thus you are subsidizing others. And there's an ancient cliché that the hen contributes to breakfast but the pig is committed to it.

You can earn an okay living in a lot of different ways, even with your own business just by *contributing*. But you can't be at the top without real *commitment*. Usually yours and those just most closely knitted to you.

And sorry about the concept of *balance*. There isn't a single person at the top of field of the industry or the community or even close to the top of the income of wealth-mountain who lives a balanced life. No one ever. No entrepreneur. No CEO. No champion athlete. No head coach if, they have a winning record. No Hollywood star. They claim it, but they might lie.

And that is what makes us different. Our happiness lies in growing and building businesses.

And yet we forget that **a business is something out of which you take money**. It is not something into which you put money. So we subsidize, because we forget.

Your father probably taught you to **pay yourself first.** Yet we pay ourselves last.

We know we shouldn't have all our eggs in one basket despite what some disingenuous famous multibillionaire says about *putting all your eggs in one basket* and watching that basket closely.

Not only is he *not* following that advice himself, having multiple businesses and multiple lines of business, but also it's not true for anyone. How can it possibly be? We know intuitively to diversify our income stream.

We know, too, that one is the loneliest number in business. We may have trouble if we have one line of products or services, one channel to develop our new business, or one person who can do a particular task. And **yet 90% of our net worth for 90% of us business owners lies in the value of the business**.

So let's talk about **business valuation**. How much is a business worth? Well, we know it intuitively. It's pretty simple. A business is worth whatever the predicted future income streams of that business are. So if a business produces a dollar worth of profit, I might pay something for that dollar for the period of years that I can expect the business will deliver that dollar.

That's the only evaluation that matters. It doesn't matter how long you've been in business, how much you're invested in your business, what's on your balance sheet, how much debt you have, how much equity you've developed, how many sales you have, how many employees you have.

Why would you pay anything for a business that does not make money, has not made money and is unlikely to make money? You wouldn't. If it were in the stock market -- you'd jump. Also I encourage you to not confuse total owner benefit with real profit.

"Profits are an opinion," many accountants say. **Free cash flow is a fact.** And that free cash flow is determined by taking all the costs including an arm's-length, third-party cost of *replacing you,* and then whatever is left over, is the profit on a pretax basis.

So what are the *multiples* upon which to determine future cash flow values? They range in every business from a multiple of less than one for an annuity salesperson's book of business, or a surgeon, or an attorney, to something over 20, 70, 100 for some internet based business with a high growth, high cash flow model.

For the purpose of this book, we're talking about small and mid-sized businesses. It's hard to find a business that will pay more than 10 to 15 times of net profit. Most of the time we see increased selling for three to five times net profits.

So for example, if the business does $10 million a year and we had to pay the business owner $250,000 a year to run it for me, for us, the shareholders, the Boards of Directors, plus a bonus of another $100,000 if he met certain performance criteria and the business has after that $1 million net pretax profit, how much would we pay for that $1 million net pretax profit business.

Every day you're not selling your business, you're buying your business, what would you pay for that business? That's what it's worth. Most of us might pay something on the order of $3 million to $5 million and how would we do it. We'd probably put down something like $1 - $2 million in cash and finance the rest with a shared risk with the owner based on some kind of earn out.

Chapter 2
Small Business Owners' Myths

You are different from your employees…or any employee for that matter. You have more guts. This does not mean you have no fear. It only means that you know what to do in the face of that fear. You have the drive and determination to control your own destiny. That is one reason you went into business.

And selling can mean a major change in that sense of control. You could be out of your element. This could make you uncomfortable. Let us then help you regain that comfort and sense of control after you sell and realize a cash infusion of Sudden Wealth™.

Let's explore the myths.

The Myth of "Just selling"

This can be a disaster. Since (according to succession planning experts and our own research) 71% of all transactions wind up in litigation, or with the seller of a business only getting the money that appears at the closing table, this figure is much more likely for the small business owner. Life happens. The lives of customers and their needs change. New owners may underestimate, misunderstand, mismanage.

Representations and warranties are in dispute. Finger pointing ensues. Mutual distrust and animosity develops. Unhappiness, frustration and remorse of the seller follow. Your health could start to decline. So could your marriage, your other relationships, golf game, whatever.

This is supposed to be a joyous time. You have earned the possibility to sit back, relax, and enjoy the ride. Now, you can really enjoy the fruits of your leveraged time and labor, capital, risks, and delayed gratification. Here is the typical scenario, SBO (Small Business Owner) is 60 and has a business with $20 million gross revenues.

The $500K house is paid for. The $1 million vacation house is paid for. There is a $1 million in your IRA or 401(k). You have been living on $500,000 per year. Your business has a 10% net pretax margin, thus your EBITDA is $2 million. The business has $2 million in retained earnings. You are able to sell your business for 4.5 times earnings.

The Myth of Your Lifestyle Needs

The myth of your lifestyle needs is that it equals your pay, or your pay plus any distributions. You may not be aware that you pay more in taxes than you take out of your business. This is an indication that your lifestyle exceeds $500,000 per year.

You have done what most SBOs do: you deduct certain expenses for travel, food, entertainment, and so forth. Perhaps there is family in the business earning a salary. So you really are living on more than $500,000 per year. But that is a mere aside.

The Myth of the Sale Price

The reality is that you are unlikely to receive your 4.5 times $2 million in earnings, or $9 million, in one cash lump sum. There is likely to be:

A note retained by the SBO, or

An "earn-out," or

Stock in the acquiring strategic buyer, or

Some other shared risk with the buyer, and

A time-demand payment, in addition to the down-payment.

For the sake of illustrations, let us pretend you can and do receive that $9 million in one lump sum. There likely will be transaction costs of approximately $1 million. The broker, or investor banker, your attorneys and accountants do not work for free. You should expect an 8-13% cost here. That leaves you with $8 million. Then tax is due.

The Myth That Tax Will Be Relatively Unimportant

As of this writing, the capital gains tax is 20%. We will not even discuss the additional 3.8% Medicare tax. You will not have to pay tax on the entire $8 million, fortunately. You have that retained earning amount of $2 million, which is like a return of capital to you, and not taxed.

But still $6 million is taxable at 20%. Poof -- another $1.2 million evaporates. That leaves you the $4.8 million on the taxable portion plus the $2 million of retained earnings. Net sales proceeds total to you:

A not so whopping $6.8 million; plus,

Your retirement account of $1 million (which is as yet untaxed at a probable 40+% rate leaving you about $600,000, and you now have no deductions; zero, nada, zilch).

So all in, you have a net liquid (spendable) worth of $7.4 million. Now if you do only live on $500,000 (and it is doubtful to be that low), how long until you could possibly run out of money? That is correct. Less than 15 years. There is no rate of return you can reasonably expect that can solve this disaster.

The Myth of Qualified Retirement Accounts

And please do not make the dangerous error that your retirement account will grow and add back the $400,000 income tax. That growth only further delays and postpones the tax and the tax rate. What will future tax rates likely be? Most do not believe they are going lower. That would be counter-historical.

So if you wait until your retirement account grows to $2 million, then the share of your silent partner, and the government, is now

$800,000. If you wait until the account grows to $3 million the tax due is $1.2 million. Nor does it matter that you take your share out slowly. The tax continues to grow along with the account size.

The Myth That Buyers Are Waiting Out There

It is sad how few SBOs lack a succession plan. Note the root word here: Success. Your succession plan is critical. It includes and begins with who the likely successor will be. Will it be your family, the employees, a financial buyer, a strategic buyer?

The next step is to build into your plan the building of the business relationships with potential successors. This may include training, improving or creating a management team that does what you do, that is, to fire yourself. This takes guts, and the realization that others can and will do what you do.

Only the most narcissistic, egotistical, self-centered believe no one can do as good a job as you. It is possible that others may do a better job. That is good if the others are in your succession plan. That can lead to a greater likelihood of succession planning success.

The Myth That Fair Equals Equal

If your succession plan includes family, then perhaps dividing the business equally among heirs is unfair. And worse, it could lead to dividing the family. This is the exact opposite of your intentions, no? It could also spell disaster for the business and your value in it.

The Myth That Selling Means Giving Up Income and Less Control over Your Destiny

The truth is that with proper planning, you will have more control over creating your future. You will have:

More liquidity,

An improved tax situation,

An increase in your spendable after tax dollars,

Greater flexibility in your timing and selection of successors,

Increased negotiating strength,

More confidence in your decisions, and ultimately,

The satisfaction and peace of mind that what you sacrificed for and built has now come to fruition.

Now you can enjoy the fruits. It is now time to harvest. You can see that not only financially, but also emotionally you can be in the position you have worked so hard to create. We can show you how to take advantage of inflation, rather than be victimized by it. You can really reduce your income tax burden. You can have your family harmony, your lifestyle and your unforeseen needs taken care of, along with your legacy.

The Myth That You Should Not Extract Much Cash from Your Business before Selling and That You Should Be Plowing Capital Back Into Your Business

The truth is a business is something from which you take money, not something into which you put money. In fact, the more cash you are able to realize for yourself, the more valuable the business to potential buyers. Of course, very few will be interested if you "milk the cash cow dry."

You should continue to nurture its growth, while padding your nest egg. Aim for that 15% net pre-tax profit. Less than 5% is a problem. Greater than 20% attracts too much competition. Typically, no more than half of the profit should be re-invested back into your business.

Then the half goes into diversification of your income streams. And one great way to extract and store cash is on a tax-advantaged basis. This stored cash needs to be safely managed. You already have substantial risk in a non-liquid, micro-cap stock: your business.

Chapter 3
How to Prepare for the Big Event

The best way to prepare is… to plan. This is not sarcastic. The number 71% is worth repeating. It represents those who receive Sudden Wealth, from the sale, or any other liquidity event from monetizing your business, and who wind up either in litigation, or not receiving the full amount, or running out of money. Ideally, to prevent yourself from becoming a member of that disasterous statistic, you should plan at least 5 years, and preferably more, in advance.

If you are expecting or receiving a sale of your business, it would help to know what your cash flow needs are in advance, what the after-tax, and after-transaction cost remainder will be, what types of income you can expect from the sale proceeds and for how long, at what inflation rate, what your tax bracket will look like, what your long-term intentions are, and how to protect your hard-earned, delayed gratification from predators, creditors, and bad actors who may take advantage of your windfall.

If you are receiving a "liquidity event", that is a big cash advance on the transfer of your business, you will also need to know if there will likely be a *hold-back*, or an earn-out provision, or a claw-back clause based on performance.

Ultimately, the *seller of a business* should ask why you are selling? Can you afford to sell? Have you saved enough plus the sale proceeds to maintain lifestyle? What will life be like after I sell? What if I could keep the business and simply work less, while maintaining income and the business value?

Once you have answered these, with the proper *outside* perspective, and since the primary thing a buyer usually is interested in is the future net income streams as well as the assets that generate that income. So, protect your assets. And protect that income stream.

However, as you think about growing your current business, it will do you little good in both the short term and the long if you generate new business coming in the "front door", while losing existing customers out the "back door".

Let me say this another way. It's less expensive to retain an existing customer or client or patient then it to acquire a new one. The existing customer is already buying from you and probably wants to buy more from you if you have more to give. Keep that back door locked. Then guard the key.

So how to protect and grow the current business income. Begin with your top customers. Do they know it? What are you doing for them? How are you recognizing and rewarding them? How much of their business do you "own?" How much cross-sell opportunity is there? How many customers have they referred? Why? Answer those honestly. And make those answers what you want them to be, if they are not already.

(Warning this is not the business development book. There are others who do a far better job than me. Here is a high level survey only.)

How to increase income? Of course, there are two ways:

First increase sales. You already know how to do that one way. Get more customers. Get better customers. Get your customers to buy more. Consult marketing and sales books and gurus. Hire experts. You already know the drill here.

Second, raise your prices. If you have a 10% net margin ($500,000) on a $5M sales per year business, and you raise your price by 2.5% right now, you will have dropped the better part of an additional net margin of $125,000, for a total new profit margin of $625,000. That results in a 25% increase in net.

Please, do not believe all your customers will balk. A very few might. That could be ok. They may be high risk, or high maintenance anyway. Even if you lost up to 2.5% of your customers, your margins remain the same, with less work. You won't lose that many. You are not likely to lose any. "*Price is an issue only when value is a mystery*" according to my friend Nick Nanton. None of us drive the cheapest car, live in the cheapest house, buy the cheapest clothing or food. Nor do they buy the cheapest widget your business produces.

We are all willing to spend what we want to spend. You have more pricing power than you can imagine, especially if you can add value.

How much would you spend to put your dog in a kennel? Are you aware there is something called the Pooch Palace? I believe it's in Ohio. It's $1,000 a night kennel where they'll serve the dogfood on silver platters literally. They've got feather beds for them and they comb them and dress them and they take really good care of them. Some people like to spend that kind of money of their dog.

There are cars that people buy for a $1 million and they never drive them. A Saudi prince has a Mercedes SL and it's *made of platinum*. There are people at the top of the pyramid willing to pay, give them what they want because Zig Ziglar said "you can get anything you want if you help others get what they want".

And diversifying your income stream, what good does it do to have two new clients and customers and patients come into your front door and anger or annoy or loose or you can't make happy those existing clients. It's frustrating. So you've got your doors wide open in the front. **Lock the doors in the back**.

Make sure that you do everything you can to keep your existing customer, client or patient. And if you're fortunate enough and smart enough and disciplined enough to be able to amass your own capital, your savings, and your own outside investments, why take on additional risk?

Your business product is not a commodity, though everything tends to get commoditized. You add value. What is your value add? Do your customers appreciate that and actually value that? If not, change to what your customers do value. If so, they will continue to value it. If the value does exceed the new sales price, increase the value. Just raise your price.

Ok. Now that we have increased our net by increasing sales, what about decreasing your business expenses. We are not talking about staff reductions. Nor am I suggesting you are not as lean possible. You probably already are. What I am talking about is finding inefficiencies in some key mostly overlooked or misunderstood areas that fly under the radar of your CFO and accounting team. Again that is another book. Check out "**Smart Choices for Serious Money**", by yours truly. It is available through Amazon or simply call our office to purchase a copy.

"Too many business owners concentrate too much effort in only growing sales -- the top line. More important is the real bottom line. Not just "profits" which are an opinion. Let's have a heavy emphasis on the more factual net free cash flow (which we will from now on call "NFCF") that you can protect for you and your family. After all, that is the only number you can sell.. And, even more important is the after-tax amount, and the after-lifestyle expense amount."

We will touch on a few basics. Most business owners do not have nor have they ever heard about the Private Capital Reserve Strategy™. Get one. Today. If you have never heard about this, or your advisors don't know how to create one, call our office for help. It takes time to build the Critical Capital Mass™. Usually between 4-11 years. (To asset protect that, you may call my office to request a copy of "***Cover Your Assets: How Build Protect and Maintain Your Financial Fortress***", also by yours truly).

Most business owners have improper or improperly funded insurances. Just in life insurance alone, I have reviewed over 87 policies recently, and every one, 100% were improper. Most also have improper or improperly funded mortgages. Improper or improperly constructed retirement plans. Inadequate tax reduction plans. Income distribution plans. Disability insurance. Asset protection plans. Investment Policy Statement. And risk management plans (Call my office for a copy of "***A Guide to Alternative Risk Transfer***").

These are areas we typically can find about 1-8% greater efficiencies. Every single year. That can add up to a big number. Imagine another 3% greater efficiency in the operation side of your $5 Million business. Add another $150,000 to your bottom line. Now you have your original $500,000. Plus we added more income of $125,000. And we helped you improve your efficiency by an additional $150,000. Your new bottom line with the same number of customers and widgets produce is now $775,000 for a new margin of not 10% but 15,5%! A *55% increase in net profit.*

You may be skeptical. So let's cut all the extra profit down by 80%. So your new net is "only" $55,000 greater. That is "only" a 11% increase in net profit. Better than the proverbial stick in the eye. You can do it. We can help.

And if your industry is like most, your company sells for about 3-8 times earnings before interest deductions, taxes, depreciation, and amortization. Let's say it is 4 times profit (that gives the buyer a 25% pretax return, typical for risk capital in an illiquid high risk small business by the way). Now your sale price is not \$2Million. It is now 4 times \$775,000 or \$3.1Million. Quite a difference.

THE SALE OF YOUR BUSINESS	
Before Summit	After Summit
+ \$2M Selling Price	= \$2.9M (inc. greater efficiencies)
- 10% transaction costs	- 10% transaction costs
= \$1.8M	\$2.61M
- 15% capital gain tax	- 15% capital gain tax
= \$1.53M	\$2.21M (or 45% more)

You may take 4-7 years to develop this, yet for most business owners, it is worth it to enjoy the power of proper preparation.

Chapter 4
How To (And How Long To) Prepare For "Liquidity"

"A business is something from which you extract money. Not something into which you put money."

If you are like most business owners, you may have started out to improve the world. You found a problem you wanted to solve, or found something lacking in the marketplace, or felt you could deliver your products and services better, by owning a business, rather than working for one.

Or maybe, you simply felt your value. Your financial reward would have a greater chance to be realized by owning a business. You may not have been aware of the great risks and obstacles to success. You know now. It is very difficult to own and to operate a successful business.

It is not getting easier. If you cannot make money at it, you are far less likely to be successful in making your mark on the world, in achieving your goals. Ultimately, the reason you are in business is to make money. A liquidity event occurs when you receive cash in exchange for your ownership equity interests.

This may be in the form of venture capital, or private equity, or an outright sale. Ideally, we should get involved as part of your team several *years before* contemplation of sale or other injection of capital in exchange for ownership. Here is why.

Your business is worth future expected cash flows, discounted for time and duration and market conditions. Equity has no intrinsic value, except on the balance sheet. Think of the equity in real property such as your house. Imagine two identical houses on the same street next to each other.

Can you tell which one has a large mortgage, and which one has no mortgage at all? Of course not! And can you tell which one will go up or down in value more with the marketplace? No, again. They will either appreciate the same, or they will decline in value the same.

So, the one with zero equity (all mortgaged) goes up or down the same as the one with 100% equity (no mortgage). Thus the equity earns nothing. On the other hand, growing your sales and your profits often includes an automatic increase in your business equity.

Let us not confuse that term with the market value of the sale of all or part of your business. So why should we get involved early? Because we have seen that simply by improving your net cash flow from your business, into your personal and outside asset base, results in an increase in your business value. And that can improve the chances of a successful cash transaction, while mitigating the risk of a less than successful cash transaction.

Including us early may help you with conventional bank financing. It may help you later with mezzanine financing, still later with private equity, and later yet with an investment banking outright sale. Businesses usually have a value, and sell as a "multiple" of profits often defined as EBITDA (Earnings before Interest Taxes Depreciation and Amortization).

That multiple can vary by geography or industry, and can increase with increasing absolute amount of profit, and increasing compound annual growth rate. For smaller businesses it can be 3-5 times profits. For larger and more rapidly growing businesses, that multiple may exceed 10.

To get more than that, usually requires the business to "go public." Accountants like to joke that profits are an opinion. Cash, on the other hand is real. Most business owners enjoy free cash flow, while the profits can lead to more taxation. It is possible to have one without the other.

Profits without free cash flow can lead to trouble. Cash without profit usually spells trouble. It is ideal to have both together, and growing. You will need a collaborative team consisting of at least some of the following:

- Wealth managers,
- Attorneys,
- Lenders,

- Accountants,
- Business valuators,
- Investment bankers, or
- Private equity groups.

With the said team, we can help position you to:

- Increase your cash flow, and
- Increase your business valuation.

Thus, we shall be increasing the amounts you may enjoy for all the hard work and risk and aggravation you incurred while building your baby. We are not, nor do we try to be, business consultants. Rather, we simply help you extract more cash from your business into your personal accounts outside your business.

And since your business is, by definition, an "illiquid, micro-cap stock", most business owners feel more secure with the increased liquidity and safety of your capital. How does that occur? We may find areas you may be losing money. This usually may occur in the form of taxes or interest or how you finance major capital purchases.

We work, in conjunction with your team, to identify tax-advantaged ways to increase your cash position. Sometimes paying the tax now can be better than paying an unknown tax rate later. Sometimes we can find tax-deductible strategies that you were not aware of.

Once you capture your capital outside your business, you want it protected from:

- Creditors,
- Predators,
- Bad actors,
- Too much going to the taxman,
- Losses, and,
- Lawsuits.

You want it to grow at a reasonable rate. You want it to be liquid so it is there when you need it. You want to understand how it is deployed, and to be able to explain it your family. You worked too hard to risk it outside of your own business, and control.

Having this capital may be in the form of our Private Capital Reserve Strategy™. It is not a product but a strategy. Having this capital may ease the pressure on the sale. Both the seller and the buyer may feel an advantage. The seller does not have to depend on the sale transaction exclusively to improve your liquid net worth.

The buyer may be able to offer more creative terms to improve the success of the transaction. This may mean you would not be part of that 71% statistic. On a more personal note, to illustrate why getting us involved early is important, let us go back to the scenario of the $20 million business with $2 million EBIDTA.

You have $1 million in your IRA or 401(k). You have your house and vacation house paid. You "live on" $500,000. And you hope to sell your business for 4.5 times EBITDA and realize that cash. OK. So you net out \$6.8 million. Add back in your qualified retirement plan (QRP) – your IRA or 401(k), after tax and your liquid net worth would have been "only" \$7.4 million.

On the other hand, you bring us in a few years early. We probably found you tax deductible contributions of \$600,000 to \$1 million each year into an asset-protected personal account. Very common! And we helped you save another \$100,000 to \$300,000 each year through your own private capital reserve strategy.

Also very common! Now each year you have an additional \$300,000 to \$1.3 million in your own personal accounts outside the business. Let us also say that we do this for 2 to 7 years (ideally) prior to your cash transaction, your liquidity event.

This leaves you with an additional \$600,000 at a minimum up to several million dollars. And we can show you how to finance capital purchases, as well as your own transaction to maximize the sale price. You are better off. And you have less risk that the transaction will fail. And if the transaction does not perform as you hoped, you still have more in your pocket at the end of the day. Now how do you feel?

I already have a "guy"

Of course, you do. Most do. However, the rules change and they change dramatically when you shift from accumulating wealth to extracting the cash and then distributing that wealth to last your life time and to fund your legacy. So that person may not be the best person now. Your tax position may change.

Your risk tolerances may change. Your goals may change. Your time horizon may change. Therefore, your advisory may need to change because, what got you here, may not get you there. Most people, who have a "guy," do not have someone who understands that distribution of your wealth to last a lifetime and longer is another story.

You need someone who not only manages your investment portfolio. You need someone who, through collaborative and comprehensive planning, takes into consideration asset protection, estate issues, tax optimization, risk mitigation, liquidity, and growth.

Someone who has been there before; who understands what the issues may be; and who has already done this countless times for others and for himself. Someone who has built, bought, and sold businesses. In short, you need someone who knows how to translate the work of your life of owning and building your business, now, into fulfilling you're the goals and needs of your life.

Chapter 5
Purpose

Be careful. Everyone needs a purpose. The biggest question for most prior business owners becomes, what happens now? After selling a company, the purpose of day-to-day activity gets blurred. You thought your purpose was to build a company, sell it and reap the benefits afterward.

Then you find that $2 million, $8 million, $25 million or $50 million is just that. All that money doesn't necessarily provide the purpose you once had. Former business owners are like professional athletes who face a somewhat similar stark reality of life after sports.

You are not the boss anymore. You do not sign the checks or decide anything else for your company or employees. In many cases, you are just like your employees, only with more money. Lack of purpose is something most former business owners do not expect.

They know there will be changes, but not this kind. The driving force to a big piece of their life is gone; poof, no more! This is typically where people discover that they must do some soul searching. What is next? Shall it be pleasure, work, philanthropy, spiritual quest or another business? Not enough to do.

When consulting with clients I can usually tell when this point has been reached. They start calling me more frequently and asking the same questions. They also start attending to detail much more than normal. The main reason is their lack of enough to do.

Many wives become frustrated during this period. They ask why their husbands cannot get an office, go somewhere, and get occupied with a community work. This juncture in the life of a former business owner becomes critical. If he has a plan, things will likely go well.

If not, he must look within and find out what really makes him tick. Occasionally, this is a first for him. Perhaps he owned a business for more than 25 years and only had to think of staying afloat. He may never even thought of why he was placed on this earth.

Having watched owners sell companies for more than 30 years, I have noticed a deep void. For many of them, purpose of the existence of their life is of no consequence. Most former owners have never even thought about the larger purposes of life.

They always fail to look beyond the important and valid purpose of running a successful business. Suddenly, they are looking at a situation where money is no object and time is no problem. Most never think of this concept as a reality, only as a theory. While consulting with business owners who have sold, I frequently hear the following kinds of questions:

Where did I come from?
Where am I going?
What's it all about?
Is this all there is?
What should I be doing now?

A new sense of purpose must be awakened. The driving purpose the owner once had is largely out the window. There now is something more important than raising a family, building a company and gaining net worth. A new sense of purpose must be awakened within him in order to have a reason for living.

What I am about to say next may sound dramatic but I believe it is true. Maybe it is just a feeling, and not true at all. Without a new sense of purpose, the prior owner may be facing an earlier death, perhaps much earlier. With new purpose, however, the former business owner becomes invigorated and uplifted to move forward.

What eventually happens for some is the realization that the business they sold is parts of the journey. The realization drew a picture of a family, business and net worth as not necessarily ends in themselves. For others, there are unlimited examples of new careers in politics, non-business professions and philanthropy.

Some would not pursue a new career but will discover that a long dormant hobby takes on special meaning. This becomes more meaningful especially when service to others is part of the equation. And let us not forget the importance of being an involved grandparent or great grandparent.

Being there for children who need us and look up to us is not to be underestimated. In the great scheme of things, many things in life can be characterized by cycles. This includes religion, business, families and nature. The main task of the seller now is to sow the seeds for a new and meaningful cycle.

Happiness—what is it all about? Happiness, like financial security, is a very relative term largely defined by the individual. Ephemeral and often changing, everyone seems to describe happiness from his or her own perspective. This chapter is written because of the angst that arises when someone sells a business thinking happiness comes.

For owners who are not ready to sell their business, happiness is getting started in a new business. For owners who were ready to sell their business, happiness may mean doing things they never thought of. This may include walking, painting, traveling, or very little. In the long run, happiness is a state of mind. And it intends to be upbeat, forward thinking and positive.

One of the happiest business owners I know lives in West Texas. Roger sold two different companies and ended up with a reasonable amount of money. He always seemed happy, even in the beginning when money was scarce. I noticed his relationship with his wife was always superior and the entire family got along well.

As Roger became wealthier after selling other businesses and moving to Arizona nothing changed. He stayed happy and the same appeared to be true of his entire family. He sold the businesses when they were ready to be sold. He also has good relationships with his employees and friends.

Actually, money meant little to him. The happiness of Roger was not built around the wrong things, such as, control, wealth, ego and power. It was built around enjoying life and positive human relationships. Happiness indeed cannot be bought.

In contrast, I had a client in the Southeast who sold a company for a very large sum of money. The children of Fred were grown and there was enough money to do anything he wanted. But he was not happy when he had the business or after he sold it.

A long and contentious divorce ensued. For five years, he was intent on controlling his soon to be ex-wife and the divorce proceedings. Fred spent millions of dollars on the outcome and still was not happy. For some reason he appeared to concentrate on being in the state of unhappiness.

Rage and revenge were his driving forces. Money was no object and he spent a lot in order to find happiness, which always eluded him. As indicated previously, happiness is a state of mind just like all other states of mind. It is not bought, but rather produced internally.

The path a business owner takes after selling his company can leave him extremely happy or extremely sad. Many business owners are happiest when running their business and managing operations. And in so doing, they have gained some knowledge or expertise.

One most poignant meeting for me is my interview with a business owner who should not have sold. He normally does not realize his mistake until sometime later. A number of owners have told me they regret having sold. They loved the day to day excitement and the sense of control they had in their situation.

Unfortunately, a larger company came along and made them an offer they thought they could not refuse. Only one problem, they confused money with happiness. When contemplating selling his company the owner is advised to ask himself a few key questions:

• Does he relish his daily routine and its challenges?

If so, then maybe he should think twice before selling. A year round vacation may not be as satisfying.

• Does he enjoy controlling a large organization and working toward long term goals?

If so, he should probably keep the company. After the sale it is mostly his family, money, and friends. His world shrinks considerably.

• Does he enjoy helping other people reach their goals?

If so, maybe he is better off with the company where he can directly help others with their career goals. In other words, selling a company is not always the right thing to do. Unless, that is, the offering price and net profit are the only criteria. When contemplating selling, the owner must remember that happiness is a super achievement.

Happiness, definitely, is not one to be taken lightly. He may be happiest managing his company. Only he can ask and answer the vital essential questions on this subject.

Chapter 6
To Sell or Not to Sell

Months, or even years after selling their entrepreneurial enterprises, many former owners begin to rethink their decision. The thought process is normal and almost all of them go through this retrospective experience at some time. Most of these reflections are fleeting in nature.

Owners, who have not sold and are finding it difficult to reach a decision, might consider some factors. In my opinion, 20% of all sellers should have retained control of their companies for two primary reasons:

Reason No. 1: Loss of perks.

First, is the loss of valuable, personal, monetary benefits or perquisites – "perks" for short. When the owner of a small company, $2 million or less, sells, he surrenders all the tangible benefits. This is because all such tangible benefits, connected with his ownership, are tax free or partly tax free.

This includes use of company autos; life and health insurances, forms of tax-deferred income; and other perks. Such expenses are always included in the expenditures of the business operations. When the small business owner sells, he usually receives a lump sum of cash or acquiring organization stocks.

Some small business owners receive a combination of the two. Creating from these assets the same life style the former owner and his family enjoyed can be difficult. I have known many owners who fail to calculate the required capital to produce a cash flow stream.

The cash flow should be equivalent to the magnitude of their remuneration, plus benefits, from the sold company. After tax cash flow is the crux of spending ability. If an owner sold without considering the cash flow, he should start searching for another business to acquire.

Age is also a key factor, particularly if the seller is 40 to 50 years of age or younger. The replacement of cash flow can be projected for another 35 years or more. And the sum adjusted to the 25% inflation rate annually, along with federal and state income taxes.

Obviously, the income stream is difficult to maintain. And the cost of living is usually higher than anticipated by heads of households. A huge pool of capital and reasonably good fortune with investments are essential. The owner who sells is often not aware of this fact until it is too late.

The proceeds from the sale of the company seem large and ample at the outset. But they shrink substantially compared with the former income and cash flow from the company.

Reason No. 2: Mental and emotional factors.

The second reason to consider carefully before making a decision to sell is both mental and emotional. Many owners do not realize how focused they are on managing the company they have created. After selling their company, they can lose their bearings, self-importance, even self-esteem.

In the beginning, they concentrate on sports, travel, and other projects they envisioned, which freedom from business allows. It may take the substitute forms of sharpening golf skills, fishing, and other avocations. These surrogate occupations may last only a few months before boredom and dissatisfaction kick in.

Sometimes, the spouse must pay the penalty for the aimless wandering about the homestead. A characteristic I have frequently observed in former owners is an almost frantic search to find something. Former owners almost always welcome anything constructive to do.

They check into business deal, after business deal, for possible purchase, franchise arrangements, consulting offers, and other opportunities. At some point, these individuals reach the painful conclusion about their tragic in selling their successful business operations.

They realize that the sold business is the essence of their lives. Unfortunately, this awakening is ex-post facto and, of course, too late to change. The sole avenue of escape and change for many is to locate another business operation available for purchase.

In so doing, they will have to utilize assets from the prior sale. This path, however, can be treacherous. Most former owners had knowledge and experience in a specialized field of construction, manufacturing, retailing or services.

In addition, most of them have signed contracts for their company sale that included a long-term clause. Usually for five years or more, they cannot compete with the buyer of their former business. The disadvantages and risks of entering a new field of business are obvious.

The above factors should be carefully weighed before an owner makes an irrevocable decision to sell his company. The ultimate decision is basically an enigma with no simple answers. A large business owner may receive huge liquid assets from a premium buyout. Yet despite that, they can still feel lost and without purpose after the sale.

A small owner may want to sell out but cannot afford to sell less than an adequate price. Owners must consider all ramifications. And the final decision may be determined by a sense of intuition. But the first and top priority question must be to sell or not to sell. It is imperative to know salient factors before deciding to sell a business. In this way, the founder of the business can be aware and do the necessary steps for the right reasons.

Can you answer the following:

1. How is the market doing for the last ten years?
2. Why am I really selling my business?
3. Aside from selling, what are my other options?
4. Who are my potential buyers?
5. At what price shall I sell the company I worked so hard for the last number of years?
6. How shall I be paid?
7. How shall I go about the selling process?
8. When is the best time to sell?
9. What will I do with the proceeds of the sale?
10. What shall my life be after the sale?
11. Shall selling my business affect my family?
12. Who may I turn to with regard to this dilemma?

These are just a couple of questions you may encounter when you consider letting go of your business. You may probably have most of the answers by the time of contemplating the sale. We, however, want you to consider the whole picture so as not to get lost along the way.

Understanding business trends is important in your decision making process. In a way, it forms part of your business forecasting. A ten-year period analysis is adequate for you to see where your business industry is headed for. Understanding the trending fluctuations will assist you in applying it to the future trend.

In so doing, you can relate the past figures to new business, technological and market changes. You may also want to consider the economic growth and forecast of your area of operation. Should market saturation be one of your reasons to sell, you may consider looking into other areas or countries to market your product or service.

Another trending aspect you may want to look into is the peace and order situation of your market. Needless to say, no business can thrive when focus of your potential market is on survival. If you see a bleak future, then it strengthens your plan to let go.

Otherwise, you may think of what changes you may need to implement in your business to continue its profitable operations. Whatever decision you may have, just make sure you prepare a proper business departure planning. This is to ensure a smooth transition for the whole business and its employees.

CHAPTER 7
Alternative Exit Strategies

Now when people talk about exit strategies, most of the time people are merely talking about the sale of the business. Here I will share with you some alternative exit strategies prior to, or instead of the sale of the business.

"A business is something out of which to take money. Not something into which we put money". Too many of us forget that.

What should exit the business first is some net free cash flow. I know we all want to put some of our profits, if not all of our profits, back into the business to help it to grow and to build equity.

However, equity earns nothing. It never has, never will, never can. What does earn something is the ability for that equity value to grow. That equity value often includes book value and is usually based on increasing the net profit.

If there *is* a million dollars worth of net profit, it would be a good idea to take out at least 10% of that net profit and diversify your income stream, if you have a high growth business. If you have a low growth business, it is probably best to take out 80-85% and diversify the income stream.

"A small business is simply an illiquid, micro-cap, high-risk, stock in which you are over-concentrated." It will serve you well to diversify early and often.

Pay Yourself first and enjoy a **Tax Free Retirement –**

We pay income taxes; and most of us pay our taxes prior to our salary hitting our bank account.

While we live on income, not assets. If you had all the income you need for as long as you want, why would you need any assets? Imagine, would you want to have all the meals you were ever going to eat for the rest of your life delivered today? That's the equivalent of having your assets piled up. What we really want is one meal at a time. That's what income is all about.

Is it a coincidence that we retire at 65 because social security starts then? The entire concept of retirement has been spoon-fed to the American public by the government and financial advisors for so long that few ever stop to ask: "Why do I want to retire?" "Why that age?" "What will I spend the rest of my life doing?"

The access trap.

Your money is trapped in qualified retirement plans, otherwise known as government retirement plans and equity in your house. Why not access your money at any time for any reason and tax free? This is only offered by insurance companies.

There are only three places where you can chose to put your money: Wall Street, the banks, and insurance companies. Financial advisors often don't understand insurance companies and insurance agents also don't understand personal finance.

Part of the reason people often miss out on the best things in life is they're holding misconceptions and falsehoods as truths. For example, you can get a cold from wet hair, if you pull one grey hair, ten more will show up. We trusted who told us this, so we never questioned it and small business owners are not worth the trouble for most retirement plan specialists, especially those with fewer than a hundred employees.

1. Small business owners have no significant retirement plan and often no exit or succession plan.

2. Procrastination is another problem; it catches up like a hungry lion. Early on your business has a negative cash flow. Then, as your cash flow improves you use it to fund your growth and finally, it's not pursued and it must fend for itself. So, you must depend on your business income or the sale to retrieve it.

3. Your business is hungry and must be fed

4. small business owners usually started their business on debt, which eats into margins and cash flows.

5. there is no time.

6. qualified plans are expensive.

7. qualified plans are a liability.

The Private Capital Reserve Strategy solves all this and more and there's the new retirement mentality. Why wait to retire to live the way you want? You lack a vacation, you long for a vacation. The history is that at age 65 you'd have a decreasing life expectancy, you also have a higher unemployment so others can fill in. That's the purpose of original Social Security. Money maturity comes from decades of saving and prudent investing.

The definition of happiness is wanting what you already have, according to Mitch Anthony. Security equals the freedom to pursue your goal. Success equals the satisfaction of reaching your goals. Financial planning equals wealth management equals:

1. Asset protection.
2. Tax optimization strategies.
3. Distribution strategies.
4. Estate planning strategies.
5. Cash flow strategies.
6. Risk management strategies.

As small business owners tend to focus only on one and then they're not even well-diversified. Diversification is like having only umbrellas on a sunny day and only sunblock on rainy days. The best way to diversify would be to have some sunblock and some umbrellas. Let us help you face the investment reality. Many think that they are smarter than they truly are, many think that they are above average, many have a track record focus, many are not avoiding and are retaining losses in the form of some cost and many are believing in some unfair advantage and many are not paying yourself first.

LUC

Ask yourself this question: Is the money really yours if you cannot access it? I spell luck, **LUC** – which stands for **Liquidity, Use and Control**. I would also encourage you to pay more attention to your **lifestyle needs** and clarity of what life will be like after work. By having those lifestyle needs met and wants under control, that will take a lot of stress off of you in your business and enable you to improve your free cash flow, your financing operations, your marketing efforts, your leadership endeavors, your systems, and make you happier.

Now how and why should you **take money out of the business**? Well we've already talked about why. It's important to take money out of the business. You need liquidity, use and control and you need to diversify your income stream. How to do it? I'm already operating as efficiently as possible, you may be thinking.

Let me give you an example. Assume a business does $10 million a year, owner benefit for $350,000 a year. Say I'm frugal, save $100,000 a year from that total owner benefit, and I have a profit of $1 million.

If I save $100,000 and I invest it, what kind of return can I possibly expect to get? Again for round numbers, again unrealistic, let's take a look at 10%. 10% of $100,000 is $10,000. What if through greater efficiencies without staff reductions your taking care of certain taxes, insurances, systems, mortgages: You're able to save just one half of 1% of your $10 million business?

Well 1% of $10 million is $100,000. One half of 1% is $50,000. If you take that $50,000 and now you add it to the $10,000 you've earned, you've just increased your returns by 600%. You now have a return on your $100,000 savings of $60,000 instead of $10,000.

<u>Retirement Plans</u>

One of the ways to take money out is through your government **Qualified Retirement Plan ("QRP")** such as a 401(k) and others. We know what is wrong with those. First, it is a payroll reduction by definition. So you are not really saving any tax. Then, the government tells you who may put money in, how much you may put in, what you may put it in, when you may put money in. All for a tax-deferral. Let's agree to change that word to a tax postponement.

Then the government tells you when you must take the money out, how much you must take out, whom you may leave it to, and oh, by the way, when they figure how much money they will need from you, they will tell you what your withdrawal tax rate will be. For people with high income needs (above $150,000 annually, per couple as of this writing), it may pose a real threat to your overall wealth. For more on this get a copy of the book: "***Smart Choices for Serious Money***."

ESOPs

What about an **ESOP,** an Employee Stock Ownership Plan? It is a form of a government-qualified plan. It is a highly regulated entity with excellent tax characteristics. However, you are still dealing with regulations from DOL and IRS. It works like this: you sell your equity to your employees; *you* go to a bank to borrow the funds for your employees to pay back, and *you* guaranty the note. Hopefully, your employees and your business are able to pay back the note.

About 6800 companies in the U.S. had ESOPs as of this writing, according to the Department of Labor. Owners get to defer (that is postpone) taxes and get tax deductions for the contributions to the ESOP. Appraisers rely on company management for valuations. This may lead to trouble.

ESOPs face increasing litigation from the regulatory authorities. Very obviously, not a happy position to find yourself. The allegations usually arise regarding the valuations. This can be very successful, especially if you are an extremely large (greater than $275 Million value) business, and very risky if you are the typical reader of this book.

ODOPs

You may have heard about the **ODOP**. It stands for Owner Debt Option Plan. And it is regulated by you. It works in a similar fashion to the ESOP without the regulatory risk: you retain the equity. You go to the bank and borrow the funds; your business makes the payments. The payment is an interest only note with a balloon in 7 years. You place the borrowed money into an asset protected low yield, low risk account, in which the money compounds tax-free. You may access the money any time, for any reason, usually tax-free.

For example, say your business has $10 million in sales, and $1M in EBIDTA, with $700,000 net free cash flow. Your business borrows $3Million. You place the $3 Million into the ODOP account. Payments for interest and principal at 7% interest will be around $500,000 per year.

The original $3Million you borrowed will have grown also to say $3.6Million in your ODOP account. If you have done this, you may have reduced the risk associated with a sale. And you have increased the total amounts available to fund your needs and desires.

Assuming your business is still growing, why not do it again? At the end of the 7 years, if you have a 10% Compound Annual Growth Rate of profit (CAGR), your profits will have doubled, along with your net free cash flow to over $1.4Million.

You borrow another $3Million and do it again. At the end of the next 7 years, your $6.6Million will have grown to say $8Million.

You still will have owed $6Million. Your profit has doubled again. You role over the note to a fixed 10 years amortizing payment of interest (at say 9%) and principal, your monthly payments will equal $76,005 (annual $912,060) with your profit now $2.8Million, $2Million net free cash flow.

Your ratios are good, your cash flow is sufficient to handle the debt, and to leave more for you to do what is best. You will have more than $10Million in your bank that you can access tax free, at any time and for any reason at the end of this term. If you could have sold your business for 6 times EBIDTA originally you would have wound up after tax and expenses of somewhere in the neighborhood of $4.2Million. And you would no longer have owned the business. This is a way to have your cake and eat it too.

Let's look at the **Personal Economic Model® ("PEM")** from Circle of Wealth Systems®, MoneyTrax, Inc. If you were given all the money your business generated over the course of that business lifespan, would you treat that money differently than you do now?

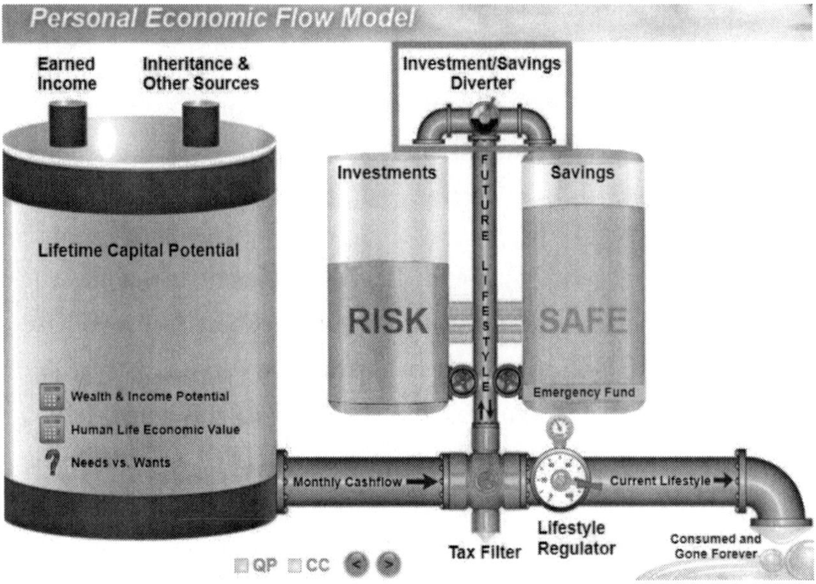

Courtesy of Circle of Wealth Sales System, MoneyTrax, Inc.

Now, I do this exercise with individual investors, retirees, and people who are employees, highly compensated employees for example. Let's just suppose you are a highly compensated employee and for round numbers again, let's just supposed that number is $100,000. Let's suppose you earn that $100,000 your entire life span. From the time you're 20 to the time you're 65, you've earned that $100,000 a year for 45 years. That's $4.5 million. We're assuming no inflation, no taxes, and no growth.

So in your life span, $4.5 million will have run through your fingers. So suppose instead of your earning $100,000 a year, someone came to you at age 20 and said here's $4.5 million. You have to go to work, exactly the same, for the next 45 years but you're not going to get paid another dime. Would you treat your money any differently? Almost everybody that I've spoken to thinks that they would have.

So let's really **scale this up**. You have a business that does $10 million a year right now. It's a 20-year old business, so we started at zero. So let's say it averaged $10,000 a year. And let's say half way between the zero and the 20. And let's say it did that for 20 years. $10 million for 20 years; that is $200 million.

How much of that $200 Million that you generated is in your bank account right now? So your efforts, your risk, your capital, your labor, your family sacrifices generated $200 million for others. Again, how much of the $200 million is yours? Are you pursuing happiness?

True profitability really means that you've generated enough from your business prior to selling your business that you could live a slightly more modest lifestyle than you are currently living, slightly. And by the sale of your business you can now exceed that modest lifestyle for the rest of your lives. The quicker you can get there the better off you'll be. The better you'll feel. The more confident you'll feel. The more clarity you'll have. The more comfortable you'll be. And avoiding the losses is more powerful than picking the winners.

Your business already is an illiquid micro cap highly volatile, high risk, illiquid business stock. If you have to generate $10 million to be able to save $100,000, and then you loose $20,000, how much more do you have to sell in your business to get that $20,000 back? At least $2 million worth of sales. **Avoid the losses**. That is more powerful than trying to pick the winners. Consistent excellence will out perform occasional brilliance over the long term.

Why not place a little bit more emphasis on creating liquidity and risk reduction and diversification of your income stream? If you need money in a hurry it would be certainly in your best interest to **diversify to liquidity**.

<u>Buy Sell Arrangements and Agreements</u>

This has different meanings. To <u>transaction experts and attorneys</u>, it is a form of a *put/call strategy*. And this keeps both parties "honest" in the pricing and valuations. It works like this:

I *put* my shares to you because I want out. I ask you for a price. You feel it is reasonable or low. You then exercise your option to buy me out at that price (and on pre-determined terms). Or you feel the price is too high. You then decline to buy me out, and force me to buy you at the high price.

In the alternative, you want to buy me out. You *call* my shares, or offer me a price I think is reasonable or high, and sell. Or your offer is too low. I can then exercise the option to buy you out at the price you offered me. This arrangement ensures both parties get fair pricing, and is used very often in estate planning.

To <u>financial and business planners</u> it is appreciably different because it is a *funding mechanism*, usually through high cash value, low death benefit permanent life insurance. This is an excellent and under-utilized tool. It works like this:

The business has profits. You and I are business partners, and our shares are, or will be, worth $1.5 Million each. We each take out life insurance on the other. We fund it with $100,000 per years for 15 years ($1.5 million over the life of the agreement).

After 15 years, the cash value is probably worth about $2 Million. We can then borrow against the policy to pay the $1.5 Million to buy out the shares. And in many cases you never have to pay back the loan, because it has enough death benefit, say $2.5 Million, to cover the loan.

The death benefit can be used in case of death, in place of key man insurance. The death benefit also often can be accessed in case of *disability*, which is much more likely than death itself in middle-age.

And even more beautifully, to the extent we decide not, or do not have to buy out one another, we have all the premiums paid at interest plus and with out tax. We can withdraw that amount for any reason, at any time, and when done correctly, completely tax-free. It really is as close to a no-risk alternative as you can get.

The reason most do not use this method is 1) because many business owners and insurance agents do not understand it, or many insurance agents do not explain how to make this work, and what the downsides are. If it is not fully funded over 7-15 years, it is inefficient. And, 2) it requires sufficient business cash flow to fund.

Most commissions come from the death benefit, and not the cash value build up. And to lower the cash flow requirements for you, the misguided suggestion is often to lower the rate of cash value build up. However, when done correctly, that is fully funded, you can recapture all your premiums, at competitive interest rates, and usually tax-free.

These arrangements are often but necessary to reserve for internal succession plans. These can take so many forms that it is too much to discuss here. For more on internal succession options, contact me.

Encapsulate Risk and Recapture Premiums through a Captive

Business is risky. What if we could insure against loss of our largest client, or our largest supplier, or loss due to sexual harassment, or a variety of other non-standard risks? What if you could recapture, at interest, all your insurance premiums? What if you could do this in a tax-advantaged manner? It is not too good to be true.

The way you may be able to do this is by owning your own insurance company. I know this sounds complicated and expensive. Perhaps. However, it is used routinely by auto dealers, as well as thousands of other types of companies, for excellent and significant net benefit.

When you do that it is called a "captive" insurance company. Because it is privately owned by you. (For details on this, please request my monograph, ***A Guide to Alternative Risk Transfer***.) This type of risk mitigation has significant advantages.

The costs have come down dramatically over the past several years due to competition. Section 831b of the IRC allows for up to $1.2 Million of tax-deductible insurance premium for business risk. The reserves grow tax-deferred.

And since you will also own, indirectly, all the reserves, to the extent there are limited or no claims against your insurance, you then may be able to access those reserves in a tax-advantaged, asset protected manner that is completely outside your estate.

This is one way to remove cash from your business, tax-deductible, have it grow tax-deferred, and then access this cash income tax-free.

Of course, you still would rather sell your business, at least at some point, correct? Read on…

Chapter 8
Can I Even Sell My Small Business at All?

How can we develop an appropriate and complete exit strategy? Is a sale the only way? It may be the preferred way in many instances. What makes a business **saleable**?

Well first of course is **sales**. How the sales have been. What the compound annual growth rate is of those sales. To whom those sales are made and how those sales are paid. How many product lines are available for those sales? All of those things matter.

Then there is **scalability**. If it's a professional services organization like an accounting firm or a law firm or financial firm or a medical firm, it's not really that scaleable. On the other hand if it's a software manufacturer, it's highly scaleable. And there are infinite variations in between.

Systems, you must have systems in place. If you need to be spending more time on your business systems, so that your business can function and operate with either fewer people or if any of your people go down for whatever reason and so that you can plug someone else into that position to help you. Because the only purpose for an employee is to do something you otherwise could not do or would not do or rather not do for yourself.

For example, you might not mow your lawn because you'd rather spend time playing with your child. You might be able to do it and you might even be able to do a better job than the person you've hired. But it's not a high value use of your time. Having systems enables you to become efficient and more effective. It gives people a clear purpose as to what they're supposed to do and how they're supposed to do it, when they're supposed to do it, for whom they're supposed to do it, and it's certainly helpful if you can tell them why they're supposed to do it that way.

And finally, a **succession plan**. This needs to include disaster recovery. Let's suppose you as the business owner are in a car accident or a skiing accident. Let's suppose you're an orthopedic surgeon and you're in a skiing accident and break a shoulder.

I know an orthopedic surgeon who was in a skiing accident and broke his shoulder. Or, what if you get sick? Or if you run a pretty big international operation--what if you get kidnapped? Or suppose you're just planning, you know you're healthy and safe and everything is percolating along just fine—what happens then? Do you just walk away and drop everything and abandon your employees and your customers and your suppliers?

After all, we do have responsibilities. You must have a succession plan in place. So having **sales, scalability, systems and succession, that creates salability**.

That helps **enhance your multiples**. You might go from a multiple of three to five to a multiple of five to seven or higher. And when working on your succession plan, most of the time when people buy a business, what they're buying is the management team. Whether it's a private equity firm or a venture capital firm, or even a strategic acquisition or financial acquisition. It is the team that you've put in place as your job to develop the proper leadership skills for yourselves and help your successors become good leaders as well.

Not only that, it is your job to do as few jobs as you can in your business. And we are all in the same business. And what business is that? We are in the business of marketing and growing our business. Each of us just delivers a slightly different widget. One of us delivers advice and another of us delivers a software program and other of us delivers a bleacher seat. But we're all in the same business of developing that business. To do so well requires good leadership skills. And in order to reduce the number of jobs that you have so you can focus on increasing the value of your business, and so you can focus on improving your own investment portfolio by diversifying.

Chapter 9
Sell or Go Public

Most businesses reach the point where outside capital is indispensable for further sustained growth. Either the business owner borrows the required funds or raises capital from the public investment market. One of the big choices that arise for the owner is this: "My business is at a certain level of value."

If I expand it in the public realm it could be huge and I could be much wealthier. If the markets go bad and I fail then my worth and greatly reduced. I know that I also could sell the business right now for a good price. The question becomes "do I take the bird in the hand or take the risk for two in the bush?"

I have seen some amazing success stories from people who decided on the public route. But they all had the personality type to be involved in a public company. One characteristic is that they not only tolerated personal scrutiny, they seem to relish it.

Business owners often dream of having their private company become a public company. They imagine their name associated with a public entity and fantasizing about the limelight that goes with it. Having access to virtually unlimited capital also comes to their mind.

I have called on hundreds of former business owners who said they could have gone public. But they decided not to and are glad they did not. I also called on a number of former owners who did not go public but wish they had. What are the pros and cons of the decision to sell to another entity or to go public?

Do these individuals have what it takes to go public? And finally, are they the types of persons to run a public company? I hope I can provide some insight into these questions.

Pros and Cons of Selling Versus Going Public

First of all, is the business owner a builder or a seller? This is an extremely important question. If he is a seller, his priority is raising the maximum amount of cash, liquid securities or both. This mindset is the exact opposite of the entrepreneur trying to build a public company.

I noticed this frequently when companies go public with multiple founders whose long-term objectives are different. If an owner has the "selling out" mindset, he will never be comfortable with the long-term view. However, this is needed to have a truly successful public company.

Taking a company to the public marketplace is a huge undertaking. It requires a complete commitment to build for the future. If an owner thinks about when to cash out, his venture would not last long in the public realm. Company XYZ was a service business put together in the Mid-South with multiple founders. They went public as planned and started to grow. I knew most of them and noticed their different approaches.

Some founders appeared to be selfish and concentrated their efforts more on reselling than on the building concept. Not surprisingly, two years later, the company had to be sold to another public company. Do not get me wrong. There is nothing wrong with being a seller or a builder.

In fact, each role has its distinctive advantages and disadvantages. But each individual must discover to which group he belongs. If he is a seller, then he should enjoy starting and selling companies. If he is a builder, going public may be the answer.

The next item for consideration, in deciding whether to sell or go public, is personality. When the company is traded in the public market, the chief executive and officers become fair for everyone. Every move is scrutinized and every word is analyzed.

It starts with investment bankers and public accounting firms. But it does not stop there. The Federal Securities and Exchange Commission keeps tabs on you along with trading exchanges and financial analysts. It goes all the way down to the smallest shareholder, with ten shares, and attends the annual meeting.

The privately held company owner must ask himself if he can handle the pressure of constantly being analyzed. If not, he probably should issue an attempt to sell his company instead of going public.

Three Options if Going Public is the Decision

This happens when the owner realizes that his goals can be met only by going public. And, as he has the temperament for thriving in the eye of a perpetual storm, his options are:

1. Locate the investment banking organization or other financial entity that can underwrite the initial public offering, or IPO. Then accomplish all the financial and legal details of the prospectus for release to potential buyers; or,

2. Seek through an investment bank a public company that might be interested in buying a less-than-majority interest. Also, be willing to leave incumbent management in place.

3. Grow his company, by purchasing another company with related services or products, at excellent growth prospects.

It should be emphasized that few entrepreneurs are sole owners of their companies with absolute control of decision-making. They can truly visualize the year-to-year and often quarter-to-quarter stresses and strains. Such condition results from a goal of consistent annual increase in net earnings of 10% or more. When the growth target climbs above this level, it can rarely be sustained of additional acquisitions. This too cannot be attained through mergers or through the development of new products and services.

The shareholders and financial analysts are invariably in the background applying the pressure with high earnings expectations. On certain occasions, the pressure comes with the overly optimistic earnings predictions. Unadmitted by most business owners, ego also plays a major role in either selling or going public.

Companies essentially go public to acquire outside capital to make money for their shareholders in the future. But I have observed companies that were operated as an extension of the ego of the founder. Many times, however, that ego will get stepped on.

The occasion may arise with the release of:

> Disappointing quarterly earnings for the first time,
> A major nonrecurring loss for restructuring, or
> Heavy losses from a key product, service or division.

A CEO may wonder "why pay this price for being public?" When the owner has a private company, his decisions are usually sacrosanct and are seldom questioned. In the public realm, on the other hand, vulnerability to adverse criticism is multifaceted.

If the ego of the private owner cannot take the constant pounding, he should tell his company. He should also forget about going public. He also must determine if he really wants to confront the strains, tensions, and many tough decisions. All this is directly connected with managing a public company.

The decision to go public is only the beginning of a tremendous undertaking, no pun intended. The maker of that decision is advised to undergo keen self-analysis in order to be certain. The question he needs to answer is if he is qualified for the task and its recurring challenges.

How important is One's Privacy?

Last but not least is privacy. Many of the high-net-worth business owners we work with are very private and confidential. I have always gone above and beyond the call of duty in my dealings with them. This is to preserve the cocoon of confidentiality we share.

The inner financial workings of a top officer, in a publicly traded company, are exposed to the public. The spotlight can be relentless. In the public realm, virtually everyone has access to the share ownership of the official. This includes his benefits, salary, and how many options he has.

His whole life in relation to his company is an open book. He has to answer phone calls and questions from people who may not appeal to him. He is handcuffed when buying stock if that stock was acquired by the exercise of restricted options. The same follows when he sells stocks.

The owner also must exercise extreme care when trading stock in his own company. This is to avoid even the appearance of acting on insider information. Such transactions must be recorded with the SEC. Also, such transactions are widely reported in the media by investment analysts who specialize in insider trading.

And, finally, he has to deal with Wall Street. This makes him just like a professional head coach or even the President of the United States. What has he done for me lately? If he and his company do not perform up to expectations he must get ready for the heat.

The Wall Street gang, not to mention the other characters in the drama, can be cruel indeed. It all boils down to size, need for capital, public or private, ego and risk. The owner must way all of these factors before siding to sell or go public. Business owners have a sense of the best way to go in the majority of cases.

Most have a keen sense of themselves and what is right in each situation. They must be attuned to what makes them tick before committing to the public realm. Socrates was right when he said "know thy self." In many cases, I have seen business owners sell out and be very glad they did.

In other cases going to the public market was appropriate. Again, the self-analysis must be incisive, insightful, and thorough before stepping off the public cliff. I have listed a number of the pros and cons of going public versus selling the private company.

Among others, this includes egos, money, successes, and pit falls. The list goes on. If all of this does not sound appealing, then the owner may decide to sell his company instead. In fact, a much higher percentage of owners of private companies sell rather than go public. They understand that it is not their style.

Others who start public companies, and succeed in the venture, go on to greatly enhance the material welfare. This also includes security of everyone associated with them. Bottom line, to sell or go public, is one of toughest choices a business owner will ever face.

Chapter 10
Letting Go?

Letting go of a business you have nurtured from the start, and had managed closely for some time, would require planning for a business turnover. This refers to the process of getting ready to transfer governance of a business to another entity or person.

Its justifications are:
• To ensure a minimal interruption in the business operations; and,
• To maintain, if not increase, valuation of the business being sold.

Generally, a succession agreement is prepared to:

1. Provide cash for the business owners;
2. Minimize business transfer dues;
3. Provide stability for the business; and,
4. Help the company owner plan equitably for his family.

Transferring ownership may be through a sale, the business going public, through donation, by estate or trust. In whatever form may it be disposed of, corresponding transfer taxes need to be paid to the government. There are also some occasions when the transfer is for a grandchild.

Skipping a generation in a bequest may cause a higher transfer tax assessment. Should this be the case, an exit plan should really be prepared beforehand. The plan will have to prepare provisions for such a contingency and will enable the heirs to proceed with the business takeover smoothly.

This is when a life insurance and trust funds are badly needed. Such investments, upon the happening of the contingent event, provide enough cash to meet required expenditures. Even when a business is on the process of transfer, it is best that the company retain its stability.

Aside from the fact that it may affect the sale or its selling price, consideration should also be made for its employees. Most of these employees are solely dependent on the salary they receive from the company. During this stage, the goal is to ensure the maximization of the value of the company.

The larger the sale proceeds, the better for the business owner. In this manner, liquidation will be hastened. The remaining cash may then be planned adequately to fund a retirement plan. This is readily materialized in cases when a business owner has decided to sell the business because he received an offer that is difficult to refuse.

If you ask me, it is more difficult to ascertain the perfect time to put up the business for sale. It is such a relief that plans may be made in preparation for such events. At this point, it would be best that the business owner hire competent professionals to assist him in the execution of his plans. Such professionals consist of lawyers, financial consultants and accountants.

It would also be most wise if we identify our potential buyers: Outsiders, or People from within. Outsiders refer to third parties, either another company or a person, not related to the operation of the company being sold. On the other hand, people from within, or insiders, consist of management personnel, co-owners, employees with stock options, and family members.

Outsider buyers may be categorized into two kinds:

- Strategic

This kind of buyer acquires businesses for a particular reason. The usual reason for their purchases is to create concerted effort and profit between the company being purchased and their existing companies. Thus, they generally buy at a premium.

- Financial

This kind of buyer acquires businesses for the sole reason of generating cash or income from business operations. Thus, they usually review in detail the financial statements and assets of the company being sold. They also assess the prevailing management style of the company being long-term investors.

Payment on the sale of business may be in many forms. Depending on the negotiation between the buyer and the seller, payment may be in cash, a promissory note backed up by collateral, stocks in the new company, or a combination of two methods or more.

At times, a buyer may request a holdback for reasons, such as, indemnification. Such requests should be studied carefully and a legal advice may be sought beforehand. The selling process per se entails a lot of paperwork, legal and accounting in nature.

The essential elements of the business sale activity are:

- Non-Disclosure Agreement,
- Preliminary and Formal Due Diligence,
- Letter of Intent,
- Purchase Agreement,
- On-site Investigation,
- Closing and Post-closing obligations, and
- Common transactions documents.

See what happens when the check clears in the next chapters…

Section Two
The Big Day is Here

Chapter 11
Closing Day, Finally

You have just signed the papers for selling your company. By tomorrow morning, the cash will be in your bank or the stock certificates in your hands. You pause to reflect on how it began and how it ended. You could be the person in California who borrowed $25,000 on credit cards to start a business. And this $25,000 is now worth $15 million.

You could be the person who bought the small company from his dad. Fortunately, you built it into a $100 million enterprise now. You could be the hourly-worker who decided to do it on your own and ended with $2 million. The stories tend to be similar. The players change and the size of the company vary.

One thing, however, remains constant. Great feelings of accomplishment are soon interrupted. The crew from the acquiring company arrives to take over are the lawyers, the CPAs, and bean counters. Now they are telling you what will be happening.

This is your new regional manager and we have decided to move your office down the hall. Your reactions may be:

Was this the right thing to do?
What is going on? Or,
I feel like an orphan.

How did you end up here? Why did you sell the company? This happens to even the finest of entrepreneurs. As businesses develop, they get more complex. Sometimes, the organizers find themselves experiencing difficulties coping with the fast changes taking place.

As the company grows, the initiators will be confronted with issues new to them. Certain management areas will require manning of people with specialized knowledge and skill which they may not possess. In cases like this, the options considered are:

1. To find outside help, or

2. To sell or liquidate the company.

Outside help means bringing in a new management expert you can transfer some of your tasks. These tasks normally are those pertaining to daily operational requirements. In this way, the founder may focus on business planning and diplomatic duties.

- The next queries that need to be answered are:
- When shall I hire the needed executive?
- How shall we go through the transition?

At this point, the business organizers should accept their inadequacies and respect the reality that the person coming in has authority. Despite that, they should realize that it was them who launched the business. Through their ingenuity, they were able to provide opportunities and a better life for the people of the company.

Thus, as the business progress, its forefathers should focus on the formulation and achievement of the company's mission, vision, business development, strategy, corporate affairs and systems building. This requires a smooth power transfer.

To concentrate on being the Top Company Man, a period of time should be given for the transfer of lesser, yet equitably important, duties and functions. Communication should also be open as this power shift shall affect a lot of people in the company.

The other option is to sell or liquidate. This move may be motivated by one of three things – succession, expansion, profit, or perhaps a combination.

Motivator #1: Succession

The lack of a clear successor is one of the primary reasons for selling. A father realizes his children are not interested in running the business or the owner has no children. With people in the company who are capable of running it, the business must be sold. This must be done while the owner is still in full command in order to benefit the most.

Motivator #2: Expansion

A second reason is the inability to gain capital for expansion. Almost every business reaches this fork in the road at some point. The owner can overcome the capital problem at certain times. But then the risk becomes too great of losing it all just in order to expand. He decides to sell. If he sees consolidation in the industry and waits too long, the price goes down. If he sees consolidation coming and sells too soon, money is left on the table.

Motivator #3: Profit

The third reason for selling is simply because the offering price was too high to resist. As a business owner, he knew what the business was worth. He may even have known within a timeframe that the business would start to decline. If someone offers more than the business is worth, the owner usually feels he has to sell.

This is especially true when public stock companies go calling. And if two or three are bidding against each other, the price can go so ridiculously high. For the business owner who has sold the company, changes will take place during the next five years. Almost every company is destined to sell at some point, either to a buyer or the public market. Like acorns growing on oak trees, falling to earth where another tree sprouts, everything has a cycle.

On closing day, it would be best that the small business owner tackle his exit checklist by answering the following questions:

1. Are you confident?
2. Have you prepared a firm succession strategy?
3. Are you credible?
4. Have you addressed internal operational disputes, if any?
5. Are you ready with your prospect's due diligence?
6. Have you completed your marketing plan?
7. Are you ready to answer the possible queries of your prospective buyers?
8. Have you hired professionals to assist you in the selling process?
9. Have you designated a professional expert to handle the marketing of your business and negotiate the sale for the highest possible value?
10. Have you prequalified your business for lenders?

This simple questionnaire will ensure your degree of preparation for that big leap. Most business owners tend to be blind to the future after selling. In majority of cases, they have spent the last 10-25 years of their life focused on their company.

Once the ink dries on the Bill of Sale, it is not over. Actually, it is just about to open another new chapter in your financial life. This is the watershed event, a turning point, and life after sale is a new territory to be explored. This book attempts to offer a bit of insight into what this territory will be like.

I have discovered the business owners seem to be a different breed from employees. They have more guts and less fear. They also have more focus, determination and self-confidence than individuals lacking the entrepreneurial spirit and drive.

But the world of owners of business changes after the sale. Most believe that the replacement executives cannot manage the business nearly as efficiently as they could and did. But that's life. When they sell their company, they also sell their power. Can they live with that?

As we continue, we will discover varied reactions to the new reality.

Chapter 12
Life Following the Closing

Most business owners feel at least somewhat lost after selling their company, a very normal reaction. When he assumes the former status, and starts groping or moping, trying to figure out what to do. He thinks of himself and the days immediately after selling. Rest assured that he is not alone in this predicament.

Most former owners are in some way doing the same thing. For my years of experience, I can offer several recommendations that might be able to help. These suggestions are to enable retired owners to sail more smoothly making the difficult adjustments.

Recommendation Number 1:

Adopt a realistic and pragmatic attitude. Yes, they were successful, perhaps very successful in founding and managing one or more business enterprises. They were also good in coping with a variety of financial marketing and other challenges.

The emphasis here is on the past tense and no guarantee of them succeeding in the future. This includes other entrepreneurial or investment undertakings. Most business owners, as a group, possess healthy egos that seldom consider failure to be an option.

Soon after the sale is finalized, some have a tendency to act impetuously and impulsively to organize. In some cases, the tendency is to be in control of another company and services, marketing or manufacturing. Sadly these impulses are without adequate financial backup or expertise to make it prosper.

I can say, to my observations and knowledge, that such knee jerk financial decisions have significant disaster potentials. This does not mean that former owners should not look for other businesses. What am saying is that they must be patient.

Their friends and family may be asking, "What now are you going to do with your life?" Most of the time, the answer should simply be, "I have not decided yet." The optimal choice with the best reward to risk ratio will appear in time. The former will eventually have the feeling that the price and operations available constitute an opportunity. And this chance, he cannot turn down. Examples of two individuals who sold their businesses then reacted in different ways come to mind.

Chuck sold a company in the Southeast and immediately decided to buy a NASCAR racing company. He had never been in the racing business and merely enjoyed the sport. For three years, he lost his entire nest egg and was not able to make his business successful. He had been set for life but it now back working again in order to make it.

Tim, on the other hand, sold his company to a public corporation. He then waited until the right situation presented itself. He moved slowly and within two years started a new company somewhat related to his old. Another two years later he has an organization that is larger than the original. Tim is still expanding and very happy. The key was waiting for the right moment and situation.

Recommendation Number 2:

Set up an office away from the residence. Get a real office. Now after ten or more years with this company, the business owner who liquidates is without management responsibility. Consequently, he brings home all of his office paraphernalia with him.

Does he really think his spouse wants him home 24 hours a day? Maybe at age 65, but not for now that he is still young and able. He has all of his phones, computer, faxes and nowhere to go. He has business meetings in the living room. The family answering machine is filled with messages.

The spouse will usually be very frustrated but will try to live with it. The greatest benefit of an office for a former owner may well be quiet time. Is at a point where reflection on his life and situation is very important. Having both a place to go and a routine are very healthy after selling.

Recommendation Number 3:

Do not suddenly become a professional investor. Though a newly acquired fortune provides easy access, to stock, the former owner does not automatically qualify as an investor. Accessibility to stock, bond, real estate, option and derivative markets does not constitute the making of an investor.

James, a good friend-client, obtained a stock quote machine and all programs to run a new investment business. Actually he knew very little about investing. He seemed to forget that investing is a unique sphere with many risks along with the rewards.

In the beginning, he traded, brought, sold and tried his hand. When visiting him the next year I asked in general about his investments. His reply was that he never turned on the equipment anymore. After painful lessons, James realized that his task was to determine how much of his money to allocate.

This should be done to various types of investment vehicles while making sure he understood the risks. Having done that, he also knew that his area of expertise lay not in making money by investing. But instead, in finding capable money managers on whom he could depend to do the job for him.

That is, reach his investment goals. Passive investing through professional managers can look like an easy and simple solution. In reality, however, there are very few people like Warren Buffets or George Soros in the investment business. Investing assets is a much slower process than most people think.

Of course, patience is very important. It is, however, only one of many prerequisites in this increasingly complex and constantly changing field. Former owners interested in active investments are strongly advised to wait for the right business to come along. Their prior experience should then prove valuable in making a wise selection.

Recommendation Number 4:

Become a shrewd investigator of and careful listener to knowledgeable sources. The active, direct investor must realize that, investing in another business, require tedious and detailed scrutiny of target. The same requirement is foremost in founding a new enterprise or in investing funds in an ongoing one.

Calling his business friends, will make them conclude that he is pressing to own another company quickly. The same goes when he starts calling deal makers. Corporate finance people and deal makers will suddenly proliferate like dandelions in the springtime.

Now is the time for former owners to listen carefully. Their best opportunities can come from being around business. They would do well to stay close to active business owners in many areas of operations as possible. These officers are often the first to learn when a business is going to be on the block.

Potential buyers, who are former owners, would not want to overlook any potential enterprise available for purchase. They should indeed look at everything but take the time to watch very carefully. They should stay in tune with related critical, economic and financial developments.

In time, opportune situations will present themselves and they will recognize it. The best business buyers and business starts, as I have observed, are quite slow to commit capital. But when the right deal appears, they move quickly. It may take a number of years to get to that point. The active ingredient they all possess is the ability to listen well. They also remember that they have plenty of time.

Chapter 13
Opening The New Routine

Before starting on the new routine, it would be best to make sure that you really are ready for it. Moving on can be such a tedious choice at times. And unfinished business can be quite irritating and troublesome when you are already in something new in your life.

If you are truly ready, you will have an affirmative answer to the following questions:

1. Have you recorded all sales and expenses of the business?
2. Have you accomplished your own pre-due diligence?
3. Have you done your business tax compliances?
4. Are your business records organized and available for review?
5. Have you eliminated co-mingling assets?
6. Have you eliminated marginal perks?
7. Have you cleaned up the Financial Statements of your business?
8. Has the annual update or appraisal of your business completed?

The new routine is a very interesting time for a former business owner. Usually this period is like a honeymoon. Much time is spent getting to know the players from the acquiring company in lunches, sessions and meetings. Most often, there is really nothing particularly notable to determine.

The best foot of everyone is being put forward and potential conflicts are being minimized. The new company may be introducing its acquisition as the new great addition. The former owner probably senses, even this early, that problems could arise.

The honeymoon feeling though causes him to say, "We will work it out." Most business owners are, by nature, optimistic. There is a tendency, in the early months after sale, to assume the kinks will iron themselves out. Sometimes what the former owner challenges are indirect changes in management style and direction.

The new routine affects the spouse as well. And more especially if the spouse was used to having most costs and jobs absorbed by the company. Most of the perks of owning a business suddenly vanish:

- Company paid insurance,
- Car washes and maintenance,
- Errands,
- Clean ups,
- Parties,
- Trips, and
- Car phones.

I have visited many offices of business owners and realized the importance of a spouse. When she walks in, and everyone knows her as the wife of the owner, she is "The Boss." The same is true with male spouses when the woman owns the business.

Generally, all fringe benefits are gone after the sale of the company. All is well that ends well? At the beginning, everyone assumes that all will end well. Naturally, everyone wants to believe this. I am frequently reminded how little many business owners know what lies ahead.

The standard comment is "we are going to fix this," abjuring that "we" no longer subsist. They haven't yet truly accepted that they are now working for someone else.

Morris was a Midwest owner who sold his business in the early 1980's. I met with him soon after the sale. He had a highly upbeat attitude about how everything was going to be great. The acquiring company had promised him the option to expand the business and do well for himself also.

Each time I visited him, however, Morris had become less and less enthusiastic. I have a standard warning to business owners. If you sell your company and be employed by the acquiring company, do not be overly optimistic. Eight out of ten circumstances, it does not work.

Morris was in this situation and failed to recognize it. After the initial phase wore off, he was shocked. 15 months later, he was in Florida with a vague understanding of how life is after selling out. The new routine impacts your customers also.

They see the announcement and notice the transfer to different bank accounts. Many of them appear to be shaken so you assure them that nothing will change. You are trying to convince yourself that this is true but, deep inside, you know it is not.

After all, no one can take care of your customers the way you do and have done well. The new routine is getting established while your primary asset, cash or stock, is sitting there doing nothing. You figure this major reinvestment problem can be taken care of later. Maybe it can, maybe it cannot.

Chapter 14
Reality Check

Reality after the sale of a business comes in different packages. The business owner who stays with the new company has one type of new reality. On the other hand, the business owner who retires, or thinks he can retire, has another. The individual who owns multiple companies, however, generally experiences very little change after selling just one of them.

The business owner who stays with the company usually takes a needed vacation, or pays off a debt. He may also contemplate on next steps, all the while trying to adjust, to the next reality. I am amazed at how business owners are surprised when two merged companies may not go as planned.

Big corporations usually buy smaller companies in order to control, grow, and run the new entity. They bought, you sold. Few corporations are run well enough to allow the prior owner to join in the decision-making growth phase. There are just too many egos, too much power, too many bean counters for that.

Entrepreneurial Companies versus Corporations

Most entrepreneurial companies are more efficiently run than large or even medium-sized corporations. Generally speaking, among the top five executives of these corporations, few, if any, have even been threatened seriously. Such threats include financial insecurity, meeting payroll, or mortgaging their soul to make something happen. Hardly any executive have faced day to day in fear of losing it all.

Lloyd was a client and former owner who sold to a public company. When we first started working together, he was jubilant about the prospects of the new combination. I told him to be very circumspect. His company may have been managed more efficiently and cost effectively than the larger acquiring company.

He was a great operator and the executive controllers of the mother company were indeed afraid of him. Lloyd was a potential problem from the standpoint of corporate powers of the new headquarters he was serving. In fact, he was more skilled at managing the company he had founded than they were.

As it happened, the company developed severe financial problems and he wisely left. As part of their reality check, most former business owners, who stay on, begin to experience stress. Here are three examples.

Sign of Stress Number 1

Accounting changes

Some of the loyal employees of the former owner come along with him. And they are soon driven crazy by all the new accounting procedures enforced by the new home office.

Sign of Stress Number 2

When a capital item needs to be purchased for a relatively small sum

The former owner discovers that a 30-year-old MBA is insisting that a requisition form has to be approved at regional headquarters. Meanwhile, the hapless former owner is confronted by a customer who is livid and, perhaps, on the verge of changing suppliers.

Sign of Stress Number 3

When the former owner realizes that his ideas mean little or nothing to the big corporation

The mindset of large corporations does not adjust easily to conducting business on other than a grand scale. At best, the former owner is likely to be patronized or treated condescendingly. At worst, he is ignored.

I am a consultant to the new company. How many times have I heard the above statement! Then only to realize the former business owner does not understand this type of consulting? When a corporation buys a company it invariably has an agenda. The former owner is put into a so called consulting role for one of three reasons.

Reason number one, part of the price of the buyout is a consulting arrangement for compensation. This often takes place because more money is needed to close the transaction. The former owner in reality does little or no consulting. As a matter of fact, the acquiring company usually does not even bother to call. People ask what the person is doing and the euphemism consulting pops up.

Reason number two, the acquiring company does not seem able to find a way to release the owner. The new owners really do not want him. They also do not plan on keeping him but they often have difficulty telling him. Customarily the main goals of the acquiring company are to get the deal underway and make smooth transition.

The former owner is a footnote, an afterthought. An example of this from 1987 comes to mind. Robert was a business owner who lived in the Midwest. Yet he sold his company to a publicly owned concern in Texas. He was classified as a consultant, as well as a director.

In many public companies, power and politics are even more important surprisingly than making money. This was the case with Robert and the acquiring company. After four or five board meetings he realized that consulting meant next to nothing. It soon became evident that the new owners were never going to listen to him. They also have no intention of changing their ideas on any subject. At the beginning of his second year the company bought out his contract and he left. I am also reminded of Scotty in Tennessee whose business was acquired by a public company. He was hired with a consultant status. The company wanted him to consult with its merger and acquisition manager when potential new companies were acquired.

After Scotty visited two of the potential acquisition candidates, he concluded that they should not be bought. He backed up his recommendation with facts showing lack of quality in many areas of potential acquisition candidates. This counsel, however, put the merger and acquisition manager in an awkward position. Three months later, the contract of Scotty was purchased and he was a consultant no more.

Reason number three, the former owner will be kept on in order to retain the top customers. For example, Paula owned a business in Denver that was sold to a public company. She had three clients who represented a large portion of her service business.

The acquiring company made her a consultant in order to keep these customers. The former owner had no office, only her home. But when two of the three customers left, the acquiring company also said goodbye to Paula. Consulting tends to be very hard for the former business owner.

He is neither in nor out but usually in an ambiguous and temporary limbo. If a business owner sells his firm and works directly for the new company, the rules are clear. He must do what upper management tells him to do. This is usually a managerial assignment, not a consulting position.

Sometimes the status of the former owner is actually much clearer as an employee, instead of a consultant. One thing is certain. The new company will run operations differently than he did. The former owner is advised to keep consulting and negotiate the most favorable financial terms for his contract.

At best, consulting is a stop gap measure before he does something else. The period spent at this position may be one to three years. Eventually, in almost all cases, the former owner moves on. This may be by choice or by the decision of the new management. Consulting for the new company nearly always looks better on paper than how it pans out in reality.

Chapter 15
Family Relationships after the Sale

After the business is sold, myriad changes affecting the family will almost certainly take place. These changes will center on two major areas: work and home. Both will need to be reviewed for signs of stress. In the workplace, the essential family adjustment depends on which family members were involved in the business sold.

If the business was built and managed by a married team, a serious family problem may arise. This is because the principal owner is used to working full time while the spouse works part time. In some occasions, the spouse may even be holding a higher position. If the business buyer retains the former owner, this is usually the only contract signed with the new management.

The spouse who was turned away generally receives no monetary compensation or other recognition of her contributions. A radically altered lifestyle inevitably unfolds for this couple. To what extent they enjoy this change depends on each specific situation and, of course, their personalities.

Family Run Business

Jeff and Bonnie was a couple in the West who had a thriving and very special niche business. When their company was purchased, the acquiring corporation kept Jeff but not Bonnie. In many ways, Bonnie had been the guiding force in this company.

She would be the person to whom most of the employees turned for guidance. She was, more or less, the glue that bonded the acquisition. The offering price was so generous that neither Bonnie nor Jeff felt they could turn it down. Unfortunately, the business suffered greatly due to the change.

But the new owners, who employed Jeff, never identified the reason. Had they retained the services of Bonnie and Jeff, the business would probably have continued its established pattern.

Children in the Business

Complications can come with adult children. Many issues will face the business owner and spouse after the sale. And most of the problems will be emotional in nature.

If adult children were involved in the business sold, another complete set of issues is encountered. The more children are employed, the greater the problems. If the acquiring company elects not to keep any children as employees, new careers must be generated. If the acquiring company chooses to employ only one of the children, this can cause family tensions. Needless to say, a host of disruptive forces can be unleashed in the family circle.

Ben owned a business in the Southeast that employed three of his adult children. All were granted positions with the new company after the sale. Three years later, two of the children had been terminated and the third moved to a different site. Ben was disgruntled with the company for breaking up his family work unit. Truth is he did not have the capability to do what should have been done in the beginning.

He should not have hired them when he organized his company. He should instead encourage them to seek alternative employment at the time of the sale. Within the home, family members experience an entirely different set of issues. What used to be the routine for a family, that owned the business, is fundamentally going through changes.

Its members do not go to work at the same time or come home at the same time. Rarely do they even meet as a family at the same time. When a business owner employs family members, a different mindset is in place. Salaries and draws are different from the practices of publicly traded corporations.

And a closely built family hierarchy is usually developed. Having observed the sale of numerous family businesses, I have noted that many go their separate ways afterward. Each member has his or her own measure of financial independence and wants something different in life. This is not necessarily bad but can lead to radical changes in family relations over some time.

A Recipe for Disaster

The major family problems arise when the owner of the business tries to help financially support other family members. Usually adult children are being supported after the sale. In my opinion, this is a recipe for disaster. If a business owner is trying to support two families, the assets needed have to be large.

I have witnessed $15 million shrink rapidly when three families were depending totally on such amounts for support. And, of course, as the principal shrinks, so does the ordinary income generated by that principal.

Cecil and his wife sold a business in California and had enough money to last their entire lifetime. The cash flow they were generating from investments was very large. As they moved along in time, however, each adult child started using the parents to maintain his lifestyle.

Over time, I met on several occasions with the parents in an effort to help them. I tried to make them understand that their own lifestyle could be in jeopardy. It might ultimately require a radical reduction of periodic family subsidiaries. My counsel was ignored and, over the long run, the children squandered the balance of the fortune.

This unfortunate result transpired because the parents were not able to tell their children to be independent. "You need to make your own money and provide for your own financial security and independence" – This should have been the words of the parents to their children.

Actually, the children are robbed of the chance to make it on their own merits and win self-confidence. In the end, everyone was damaged. This family financial tragedy occurs and reoccurs repeatedly. So what does the owner do? If the business owner has children or a spouse in the business, think about the consequences of selling.

As much as possible, let everyone in the family realize how his life might change after the sale. And that the change is of a financial character. They may or may not have jobs. Their salaries may or may not be the same. If possible, make sure that the mature children know in advance that they will be on their own.

If this is difficult to do, the former owner is advised to tally the benefits of such tough love. One benefit may be preserving the new lifestyle of him and his spouse or partner. Another for sure will be his own mental and emotional health. The owners are urged to make detailed plans for the use of the increased wealth. These plans should give emphasis on how the children fit into those plans before selling his company.

Chapter 16
Emptiness

Business owners often get so caught up in the acquisition deal that just about everything else is forgotten. After all the sale hype, the business owner walks away with millions of dollars in stocks or cash. For the first time in his life since childhood, he is debt free, job free, and responsibility free.

From the outside, the scenario usually looks like a no-lose situation – the company is sold. With adequate capital for a lifetime of total financial security and freedom, what more could any person want? But somewhere in all the excitement and confusion is the heart of the seller.

This formerly successful entrepreneur is supposed to be on top of the world. But inside him, there is often a feeling of emptiness and a sudden lack of goals and purpose. The emptiness stems from once having everything to do and suddenly having nothing to do.

The contrast between his former life and his present life can be quite dramatic, even stark. In some ways, this stage of life is not too different from graduating from high school. All of your friends are going in different directions, attending different schools, and taking on different jobs.

At first, you do not know exactly what you want to do. Somehow you decide, and off to some university or job you go. You are back on track. When you sell your company, most of your friends are still running their businesses or have jobs. Somehow, you will need to get your bearings in this situation also.

A cautionary tale: Mike was an owner in the Northwest who sold his company and stayed on to run the business. His case is a cautionary tale of being heartbroken because the business was no longer his. He had only a high school education. The business had been his entire life. After selling he became very despondent and had tremendous seller's remorse. Running the business for someone else became so frustrating that he eventually quit and moved south. I do not think he was ever truly happy afterward.

Getting out of college sometimes produces a similar feeling. You have reached a level that is now supposed to make you and everyone else very happy. But this concept is a tough sell to a graduate who is 23 years old and jobless. The business owner, after selling, often feels emotionally drained, even depressed.

He expected this hour to be his happiest. However, a death of sorts has occurred. He finds himself in a period of mourning a profound loss of purpose, focus, identity. A new part must be developed in order to regain these feelings. No spouse, second home, unlimited golf, or extended travel will fill this void.

Why does he feel this way? This question is asked over and over again. He knows this hour should be his happiest, but how happy is he in his heart of hearts? In the mind of the business owner, who sold the company, lots of new thinking must take place.

This will be a time to look at himself and truly take stock. What do I like most? What types of activities get me excited? Fishing, golfing, and tinkering go only so far. After a period of time, the person usually begins to determine his new purpose in life. He then analyzes his personal concept of happiness.

For some, the sale of a business ushers in the opportunity for a spiritual awakening. During the push and pressure of running a business, there had been precious moments for reflection and contemplation. For others, the sale signals a seismic shift in focus and energy. Where what had previously been hobbies and avocations, take on a more central role.

Chapter 17
100% or Nothing at All

Business owners will often sell one business and after some time reinvest in another one. One of the nagging questions is: What percentage of their time should they invest in the new business? The optimal scenario would be to own a company and spend 30% to 50% of time with the new entity.

This would allow the owner to enjoy the fruits from the sale of the first company. Concurrently, he may have some goals to achieve and regular involvement in management decisions in the new venture. After toiling for many years to develop and sell the first business, the former owner would appreciate a break.

Surely, he would not want to become immediately locked fulltime into another. Obviously, he has the option to invest in a company and hire other officers to exercise daily oversight. Yet, despite that, he would want to retain chief executive control.

Unfortunately, in the real world, this does not usually happen. As a prior business owner, he knows that it rarely runs right, by his standards, without his presence. When their own money is not on the line, employees do not usually perform as an owner would.

The owner is the boss, or not the boss, there is not much middle ground. If his employees know he is not there most of the time, this fact has an impact. The organization that was sold had the style and flavor of the former owner written all over it. If he is not there, the flavor either does not exist or is very hard to detect.

Frank was a client in the Northwest, who sold an industrial company and shortly afterward bought another company. He would fly into town and work at the company about a fourth of the time. He became upset when employees did not know his ownership, or did not treat him as the owner.

All they knew was that his fulltime manager signed their checks. In their eyes, the manager was the real boss. In theory, the part-time system sounds great, but often has serious limitations in real life.

Marcos was a client who sold a company in the Southwest. Soon after, he bought another company in California. His idea was to have a corporation providing reasonable income in order to offset incidental expenses. Yet, he also wants a business that would require a limited number of hours and no rigid schedule.

When we reviewed his new management arrangement, he admitted the upsetting dilemma of entrapment in fulltime employment. Within two years, Marcos had sold the company and was back to square one.

Two Types of Situations Can Work Well

What does work? Two types of situations come to mind that I have observed to be generally satisfactory.

First: If the former owner had a long-time employee who knew the business well, this could be a starting point. Two ingredients must be in place:

1. The employee-manager should be in the same type of business in the second venture as in the first.

2. The employee should own at least a small percentage of the new business.

In this manner, the former owner can own controlling interest and not necessarily be there all the time. This can be a great set up.

Alan was a client in the Southeast, who sold a company and retired, or so he thought. After searching for years for another business, he was unsuccessful in finding what he wanted. In the meantime, his former top manager and two supervisors contacted him to offer him their services.

As his new business is essentially the same as the old one, he accepted their proposal. The business then worked like a dream. All the key ingredients were there: Same business, same employees. The only difference was a small investment by the former owner. Alan did not bet the farm the second time around. He let the new management bear the brunt of corporate expansion.

Second: Another type of situation that sometimes work well, is when the former owner invests in two companies. He must know well the industry yet acts as a board member only. This has been a satisfactory arrangement for many investors.

If they know the business and the people involved, then it has a chance of working. This allows former owners to invest in two companies but still exercise influence on major corporate decisions. If the above conditions do not apply, great caution must be exercised.

Both of these scenarios have some limitation, however. Not being 100% involved is a difficult role for a former business owner. This difficulty exists even though the goal would be a part-time management. More often than not, the investor or owner either has to become involved fulltime or not at all.

You cannot just dip your toe in the water. Typically, the former owner would like to run the business on 20-hour weeks. But he knows instinctively that the business world demands more. Actually, most former owners are eventually happier if they get back into the saddle on a fulltime basis.

It is in their bloodstream, as they usually have to admit, and very hard to eliminate. This is another reason why an individual, who sells his business, needs time before going to another business. And a word to the wise: If the former owner is not prepared to put in time and effort, then he should remain retired.

What have I become—*leapfrog, butterfly, beaver, or lemming*? After selling a company most business owners select a direction or style of business activity based on personality. Over the last 30+ years I have noticed four different types of approach.

In categorizing these sellers, I also noticed they resembled certain animals. Business owners usually sell their company for cash, stock, notes, or a combination of all. The newfound wealth is either very liquid or semi-liquid. Post sellers tend to either invest conservatively or spend wildly.

There usually is not much middle ground. I have discovered that the four categories of the personalities of post seller: Leapfrog, butterfly, beaver, and lemming.

Leapfrog—the leapfrog is the owner who sells the company but wants to go for more.

He sells the company for $5 million but needs $25 million to feel he has made it. To pull this off takes a big leapfrog maneuver. Some entrepreneurs can do this but the risk is high. The individual who achieved success and wealth in one business now is facing the challenge in another.

Many people have the mistaken idea that making the next leap will be easy. Most leapfrog types are very enthusiastic after selling a company. They see the huge windfall of making money with money. Most leap frogs though will end up less wealthy and dismayed over the rapidly accumulating risk laden losses.

For example: Larry was a former business owner who could have lived comfortably on the income from his investments. He personally signed notes for shopping centers trying to increase his wealth. The notes were called and he lost it all. If anything, this frog took a great leap backward.

Mack, on the other hand, was a fellow in the Midwest who sold a company. He managed to turn $2 million into $15 million through buying and operating other companies. He ensures that all his investments work both ways.

Butterfly—the butterfly is the owner who plowed all his assets back into the business. He carefully and patiently wound the cocoon of assets over the years by keeping a low profile economically. All of a sudden the business is sold and a spring-like atmosphere blossoms.

The former owner and spouse start to enjoy life a bit more. They spend some money, and become butterflies just released from the cocoon of ownership. I am always happy to see this type of owner really start to have some fun. He normally will invest in reasonably safe ventures and simply enjoy the ride, or, in this case, flight.

My favorite butterfly is Barry in the Midwest. He exchanged his company for stock in the acquiring firm. And as luck would have it, the stock increased 500% in price—amazing. He then quit working and started traveling. He gave money to his children, church, and friends and made his life one big enjoyable trip. He has continued to enjoy the financial fruits of his labors over all the years I've known him.

Beaver—the beaver is the former owner who, after selling a company stacks all the proceeds of the sale in the money dam and waits for winter to come. He tries to have everything in place for a potential catastrophe, all of the money hoarded for the rainy day.

Most beavers forget that life is a journey meant to be traveled, not placed on hold. A few beavers are happy, but most others never really enjoy the fruits of years of sweat equity. Are they really happy? Many are not and continually look for the key to happiness in having enough assets.

Sam was my idea of the never-ending beaver saga. If you have ever watched or studied beavers, you know they go from dam to dam. This is because of high water and washouts. They never seem to get comfortable, appearing to constantly obsess, if beavers can obsess. They are always preoccupied about the demise of the dam they toiled so hard to build.

Sam sold his company but never seemed to enjoy a penny of his hard earned money. He told me of his need to achieve more wealth, but primarily worried about losing what he had. As I observed Sam, over the course of time, he appeared to be living totally for his money. As fate would have it, Sam lost his shirt in his second business investment. He was so fixated on the thought of losing it all that ultimately he did. Have you ever noticed that what a person thinks is often prelude to what ends up happening? It is sometimes called a self-fulfilling prophecy.

Lemming—the lemmings are the business owners who sell their companies then take too much advice from others. These people follow each other into the sea of destruction, as lemmings sometimes do, only to drown. The lemming type of post business owner will take advice from his:

- CPA,
- Attorney,
- Insurance advisor,
- Financial planner,
- Stockbroker,
- Banker, and,
- Even his brother-in-law.

Unfortunately, none have built a business, met payroll, or seriously concerned about the loss of all their assets. I have seen lots of lemming type business owners in poor financial condition from taking much good advice. Because business owners are often good at determining what is right for them, they should trust their instincts.

As brilliant as most business builders are, they usually end in one of these categories. The greatest attribute of entrepreneurs is their ability to adapt to changing circumstances. If they do make errors after selling they can usually learn quickly from adverse experience. To shorten that learning curve, of course, is to find a reputable financial advisor with a good track record.

Section Three
Issues

Chapter 18
What If I Already Sold, Now What?

Remember that the best time to plant a tree was 20 years ago? And, that the second best time is now? We cannot change the past just like we cannot control the weather. But, we have helped business owners who have already realized their sudden wealth spurt.

And we may be able to help you. We may be able to help position you to be certain you will not run out of money or lifestyle before you run out of time. We are strategy-and-systems-based, not product-based. There are only a certain amount of and type of product available.

And taking on outsize risk in hopes of achieving outsize returns is not what we do. It is not what our clients seek. If you seek that, we are not a good fit. We manage hundreds upon hundreds of millions of dollars on behalf of our clients, who want their money safely managed to achieve solid growth.

If you seek trusted advice, that is what we provide. If you seek a collaborative and comprehensive approach, we are for you. Here is an example. Jim sold his business and netted out $11 million. He also had another $1 million in government qualified retirement accounts, and personal accounts of $1 million.

His houses, worth $2 million, no longer have mortgages. His net worth is $15 million. The children of Jim were just starting out in life. He wants to enjoy helping them more now when they really need it, rather than later when he is gone.

His taxes are through the roof. He wants to maintain lifestyle and is concerned about future taxation, and the potential for inflation. He is still worried, even with $15 million, that there may not be enough to maintain his lifestyle of $600,000 per year.

Not your, not mine, but his lifestyle, which I will grant you, is large. But still, it is his lifestyle. And all the simulations indicated that his worry was not entirely misplaced. There is a small percentage chance that he is at risk. We were able to do cash flow projections by using certain strategies and repositioning assets.

It showed how we could eliminate any risk of reducing lifestyle, including the ravages of possible long-term care expenses. And we were able to provide him sufficient liquidity to make gifts to his children and charities now, while he could enjoy making those gifts.

And we were able to show how he still could leave a legacy worthy of his sacrifice and hard work and value systems. If your number is $3 million, or if it is $50 million, we may be able show you how to improve your position. It is about process, not product. And it is about the confidence to know that what you have built is solid and sustainable.

Chapter 19
Navigating the New Life

After selling a company, very few business owners have a roadmap for their immediate or long-term future:

1. A roadmap is hard to come by if they do not know their destination.

2. They need to stop and think about the size of their assets.

3. They need to evaluate the adequacy of their assets in coordination with career or retirement plans. Consideration should also be made with the requirement for minimum investment income for any selected style of living.

Roadmap Factor Number One – **What Makes Me Happy?**

In the first place, many former business owners seldom have ever stopped to ask themselves what truly makes them happy.

Is it engineering, managing, building, having free time or a combination of all these? Aaron was a 50 year old owner of a textile business in the Southeast.

He managed the company for 12 years and made a substantial profit at the time of selling the business. Prior to buying his original textile business, he had worked for a competing company. I visited with him on two occasions. After the second visit, I told him he would probably not be an investor with us.

"Why do you say that?" he asked. My reply was that his passion in life is running his own company. He would buy another company, and therefore, would need to keep his assets in cash or equivalents. Sure enough, it happened within two years.

You also may be inclined to be a builder or engineer. If this is the case, your spouse may be in for a long, painful period. This will last until you get another company in the construction or manufacturing sector. Stu was a builder of machines in the Midwest and had many patents in the company he sold.

After he sold the company, I met with him and his wife, and set up an investment plan. Its purpose is to secure a comfortable retirement. In the back of my mind though, I had a strong hunch he would have problems. And these problems will be due to his insatiable appetite for building things.

He assured me this was not the case, so we put his money to work for a conservative future. Just as I had suspected, however, Stu started a new company within three years under a schedule of four payments. Ultimately, we had to liquidate many of his investments for this business.

After his financial obligation was completed, he had very little liquidity left. But he was fully aware of his new career and objectives, and he was happy with them. This move was carefully planned, not a spur of the moment decision. Other business owners know that, retirement from day to day business, is what they want. They want no employees, no payroll, no taxes and no lawsuits.

Bill is a fine person with whom I have done business for 15 years. He moved to Florida after having sold a company in another state. He loves every day and, he and his wife, plan everything around their leisure and recreational activities. Leaving the business world behind was great for Bill. Playing golf, traveling and cultivating friendships are, after all, his passions. I could sense this immediately about him and later verified that it was true.

Roadmap Factor Number Two – **What is the Size of my Assets?**

The second main aspect of navigating the new life is size of assets. A business owner may take $200,000 to $600,000 annually for personal living expenditures and not even realize it. Most people do not fully appreciate the benefit of being able to produce large cash flows each year.

Few business owners stop to think about what size of assets are needed to produce certain income levels. Our partnership has always categorized owners after a sale based on the size of their assets. The following are the eight basic sizes of assets levels after selling a company:

1. $500,000 to $1 million
2. $1 million to $3 million
3. $3 million to $10 million
4. $10 million to $25 million
5. $25 million to $50 million
6. $50 million to $100 million
7. $100 million to $250 million
8. $250 million upward

Roadmap Factor Number Three – **How Can I Coordinate my Assets?**

This brings us to the third area of navigating the new life. How the assets can be coordinated so that a variety of future needs are taken into account. If an owner sold his company for $3 million, he may have trouble producing his usual cash flow.

Our experience has tracked certain characteristics of the different levels. Here are some thoughts about each of the eight levels. A very high percentage of sellers, for $1 million, spend the money in a brief period of time. Out of necessity, he will have to return to the workplace in some capacity.

The $1M-$3M sellers will have to be more frugal than expected due to their accustomed lifestyle. The business produced more cash flow than their assets will. After the sale of assets producing $3M-$10M, the former owners will be able to produce a cash flow. From investment income, the produced cash flow will be equal to their lifestyles as entrepreneurs. Even so, member of this group need to be prudent. If they make one or two sizable bad investments their actual and emotional financial security may shift dramatically.

Sellers who receive $10M-$25M from the sale, should have a life of comfortable living. This is provided they do not invest a huge sum of their cash assets in one security. This applies to securities which may collapse in value before the investors can liquidate.

Problems in this category usually occur when the individuals were concentrated in investments not well researched and analyzed. I have witnessed the fortunes of people drop from $20M to $5M due to a single risky investment. The sellers of company assets in the range of $25 million to $50 million are fewer in number.

Usually, they can absorb a couple of serious investment mistakes. The magnitude of their assets generally allows time for recovery, provided future investment decisions are conservative. The number of sellers who receive from $50 million to $100 million is smaller still.

At this level, the sellers understand that taking risks is no longer necessary. What else can they buy? If they want more money then, it is the game that matters, not the money. Those sellers who receive $100 million to $250 million for their companies are few and far between.

Consequently, they can demand and pay for the best of services and goods. They know the power of their fortune, even if they downplay it. Many of them tend to make life very simple again. Company owners, liquidating at $250M and above, are so low profiled that information about them is rare.

We occasionally meet them through referrals or private transactions. Privacy becomes very important to this group. Cash flow becomes a reverse problem. Where do they invest it? Each seller of a business should realize that adequacy is relative.

What constitutes enough is different for each person. Navigating the future will depend heavily on the total value of assets at any given time. Each seller would do well to think about that concept and require periodic review. Much time, considerably more than most business owners realizes, is needed.

After selling a company, time is needed to decide on what to do and when to take action. The seller is advised to take his time. He should keep his mind clear and carefully consider all facets of every major monetary decision.

Chapter 20
Advice for the Windfall

The subject matter on counseling clienteles, for monetary boon, reminds me of a pun that sometimes is shared among those in the asset organization groups. A wretched individual, who we will refer to as Joe, is being questioned after three years of winning a $5 million sweepstakes.

"Joe, just three years ago, you won five million bucks, and now it is almost gone. Where did the money go? What happened?" Joe answers, after thinking of it for a few minutes, "Well, about half the money was spent on gambling, women, booze, and partying. The other half…well, I do not know. I guess I just wasted it."

Irresponsible, you may say, but even a judicious and smart client experiences financial loss when he is not equipped with a well-planned monetary strategy. Receiving large amounts of money, which you did not work for, can be life-changing.

This overwhelming event can plunge a person into tremendous challenges, personally and emotionally. He will definitely be experience difficulties in coping with his instant wealth. It is imperative that financial advisors handle such accounts with a personal touch.

This can be quite challenging for the chosen financial advisor as it would require reassuring the client that he need not change the lifestyle he is accustomed to. Making the client realize that however rich he may be for the moment, he may still be back to his old state, if he fails to manage his wealth properly.

Studies have proven that a large percentage of lottery winners end up being bankrupt after a couple of years. Upon failure to avail of the professional services of a financial advisor immediately, this statistic is proven true. It is imperative that the client make any significant commitments to live simply until a complete financial plan is drawn and in force.

Financial advisors should also ask the client, whether or not wealth decisions, be made by himself alone or with others, such as spouse, children or parents. At the end of the day, it had always been found that liquid unearned money is easier to spend than hard earned wealth.

To counteract on the normal wish of such clients to splurge, immediately ask them how much money they like to have after five years and when they reach sixty five years of age. Tactfully remind them that new homes and expensive items cost a lot of money to acquire, maintain and insure.

They have to understand how important is your professional advice about their lifestyle which they can afford to maintain for a long time. Wealth is a delicate subjective matter. Support your clients to keep it that way and employ considerable secrecy in the fact of the instant wealth.

Aside from protecting his and his family's safety, it can also be tough resisting the demands of friends, family and other freeloaders. There is a deluge of perplexing matters that the nouveau riche should handle immediately. This should be accomplished in its entirety.

Important pecuniary issues needing careful review:

- The way of life your clients wish to have being rich;
- The importance of a complete strategy to acquire and sustain the chosen life;
- Focus on budget for spending, donating, and giving away, rather than investing;
- Diplomacies for probable expenditures, such as, another home, educational funds and children support;
- Income target to meet desired lifestyle; and,
- Formulation of an acceptable investment device that will earn the target income.

Discourage your clients from any sort of "alternative" investment, such as private ventures, investment schemes, and so-called business deals. Seek to get their full trust so you can assist them more fully in attaining their new goals in life. Make them understand that risk management should never be overpowered by excitement of certain business concept proposals.

Find a creative way to explain to them how painful it may be to be in the position to watch wealth collapsing. And if, at times, you may not agree with them, that is because you are just performing your duty: To protect their interest at all probable cost.

Some of exciting ventures do turn out well. But the risk should always be lower than the potential reward. Your role is to prevent the client to learn business the hard way. The new rich client should understand that he has a very heavy responsibility due to his instant wealth.

It must be clear to him that he has the sole responsibility of managing his wealth. Your role is to guide and assist him being an expert in this field which he is extremely new at. As they say: "Too much money is too much responsibility." Learning this new job takes time.

I will also require, from the client, a high degree of discipline and control. Assure him that, ultimately, it will serve him well. When a person fails to gain proficiency, on effective financial resources management, it will lead to the erosion of wealth.

This is a sure event which will depend on the person's level of expenditure, amount of wealth on hand, and the squandering time. The most valuable predicament of the nouveau riche is who to select among the many financial advisors.

Clients, who are naive with monetary and financing stuff, surely can use the assistance of financial advisors in assisting them in various ways. In search of assistance for sudden wealth issues, help may be had from the many professions in the financing consultancy circle that are extended by various organizations.

Though belonging to the same industry, each professional has their own niche of expertise and degree of credibility. These professional are: licensed financial planner, investment management analyst, public accountant, and retirement financial advisor; and, commissioned financial analyst and consultant.

Consultative relationships are basically personal. It is, therefore, important that clients are at ease with their consultant. It is best that the client trusts him and is interested in his advises. In return, the client must understanding the totality of the service his advisor gives him and its added value.

There must be mutual exchange of data between the clients and the advisors to create a good and lasting relationship. The advisors should be fully acquainted with the client. On the other hand, clients should appreciate the responsible service extended by the advisor for their good and why.

After all, an advisor's intense and genuine concern, in putting in time and effort, to grow the client's pecuniary capability is vital to both parties. In so doing, a trust-based relationship is created. Consequently, it will help the return prospects, risk calculations, cash flow and salient matters are attuned to desired end results.

We have listed several links below to assist you and your clients further:

www.adviserinfo.sec.gov

www.nasaa.org

www.finra.org/Investors/ToolsCalculators/BrokerCheck/index.htm

www.sipc.org/who.database.cfm

www.sec.gov/investor/brokers.htm

http://assets.aarp.org/www.aarp.org_/articles/bulletin/money/financialquestionnaire.pdf

Chapter 21
Myths for Each Type of Sudden Wealth™

There are six myths governing Sudden Wealth™:

1. I have an advisor who can handle my Sudden Wealth™.

The truth is that most financial advisors are what we call accumulation-oriented. You may have heard this before from them: "How much do you have and where is it? We can do better!" Very few specialize in distribution planning, tax optimization, and asset protection planning.

2. I have plenty of time.

The truth is that time is the enemy of recipients of Sudden Wealth™. This is all the money you are likely to have forever. It must last your lifetime while withstanding inflation, taxation, market fluctuations, unforeseen needs, planned obsolescence and maintaining lifestyle.

The longer you wait to identify the proper distribution planning specialist, the longer you wait to plan. This results to greater risks. The timing of many of the risks is beyond the control of any one who receives Sudden Wealth™. Then the choices are beyond your reach. Having the ability and control to make proper choices is empowering, satisfying and comforting.

3. Things will take care of themselves.

The truth is that it is true, but not for you. If you let others decide for you, the results could be devastating. That is one reason that 71%, according to the experts, end up in unhappy positions.

4. I will live on less.

If that is so, why not practice living on less right now? See how it feels. What if you did not have to sacrifice? What if with proper planning with a distribution expert, you could maintain your lifestyle?

5. Planning is expensive.

The truth is that, not planning can be very, very expensive. Well, we cannot have plans until we execute planning. And there are many creative ways to keep planning cost the minimum. Many will help you plan on a contingency basis. That is planning based on the premise that you will do business in the future.

6. I can handle this myself.

The most dangerous myth! The reality is that we live in the age of specialization. And the more you have, the more complicated your life gets, and the more risks exist. Everyone wants a piece of your wealth: the government, charities, family perhaps, litigators, predators, creditors and bad actors. Not to mention the many other unforeseen factors that affects the stability of your financial standing, such as:

- Markets
- Inflation
- Economy
- Natural disasters

Chapter 22
Most Common Sudden Wealth Mistakes

A mistake is defined as an action or judgment that is misguided or wrong. Sudden wealth refers to situations when people acquire money unexpectedly. In situations like this, people tend to be overwhelmed. This is more so when it is their first time to possess such amount of money.

To assist you sail smoothly over the waters of sudden wealth, we compiled a list of common mistakes. We also included their possible solutions which you may use or share with your acquaintances.

Not knowing the difference between wealth and status.

Wealth is more about having a lifestyle based on the stability of both expenses and any produced income. Prestige transcends expensive cars, extravagant vacations, designer clothes and going out with people of high society.

From the get-go, a sudden wealth recipient has to define their financial priorities and values. So, in your current lifestyle, what facets demand the most financial consideration? An honest response will establish understanding of the image you are trying to portray.

Conserving your windfall and not spending anything.

Some people, fearful of making many unnecessary expenses, do the opposite of spending, and instead, save each penny. With wealth comes greater responsibility for them, instead of looking at it as a potential additional revenue source.

It is highly suggested that a certain amount be appropriated for yourself so you can spend it guiltlessly. It is all right to spend but start off with an amount that fits your needs and portfolio.

Not diversifying your investments.

If you keep your investments in one lot, you may not notice when investments are not looking great. It is still advisable to broaden the horizon of your investments but in a conservative way. Work with a financial advisor who can help you broaden your investment horizons. In this way, all investment decisions are made conscientiously.

Buying a beautiful and expensive home right away.

The idea of a new, immense home is one of the first things people with sudden wealth consider. We highly suggest that it be best to delay it. Such purchases may have negative long-term effects on your financial security. It is generally considered as a frozen asset. Weigh the effects of a large cash outlay on a home acquisition before making the purchase. It would be good to delay, for at least a year, making the decision to purchase a house.

Not forming new spending habits.

Before sudden wealth strikes, people are used to making expenses based on their income. But when a large amount of money suddenly comes, some people feel it will never run out. Such an overwhelming feeling encourages the person to keep spending. Sadly, it does run out and quickly too!

That is why you should adopt new spending habits, especially if your current habits are not healthy financially. Make sure you set rational spending limits, and create a disciplined spending structure for any and all accounts. And, if possible, do not quit your job until you can live the lifestyle you need or want.

Giving gifts to family and charities early on.

When you give away money to family and charities, it is considered an expense or a dead investment. Thus, it is advised to refrain from making any donations until you have made your long-term financial plans. When return of investments are assured and realized, that is the time to consider making donations or gifts.

Failing to consult with financial professionals.

If you do not create a long-term financial plan to maintain your lifestyle, you expose yourself to risk. It would be best to consult a financial advisor to assist you in making long term plans. They, after all, have adequate experience in the realm of financial management. Consequently, they are in the right position to create or suggest the right plan for you.

A hasty decision-making process.

When there is external pressure, the tendency to make hasty decisions is great. This often times lead to wrong decisions. No matter how great the pressure is, it is best to find all ways to delay making decisions. If the pressure persists, make no promises, loans or gifts.

Take a time-out to get some advice and consider all options on whatever is causing the external pressure. At all times, protect your investments and do not allow anyone to make your financial decisions. Beware of situations which easily lead to acquisition. Be wary of unnecessary kindness, poor speculations, and spending more than you earn.

If you can recognize these mistakes early on, you stand a better chance to overcome the perils. Do take precautions. It can make all the difference when ensuring your financial security and stability.

Chapter 23
Have I Got A Deal for You

One thing is certain for owners after selling their companies everyone has a deal for them. This new found wealth brings out all the deal people. Hypes such as 50% on this and double your money on that abound. They all have the right answers for investing the new wealth.

If the sellers will just entrust them with their fortune everything should be fine. This is the standard pitch with variations on the theme. Oddly enough many former business owners go for it. Having spent their entire work life building net worth they re-invested in three weeks.

I am constantly reminded that former owners made their money by founding and/or investing in business operations. They had always ensured that they had or acquired considerable knowledge and expertise on such businesses. Most of the money that business owners made was from their business.

Investing in effect, in themselves, was the logical and successful choice. New money will always attract people. Like moths on a summer night they swarm to and circle the light bulb. Amazingly, wheelers and dealers, not to mention relatives and friends, will find the new wealth.

This is despite how hard those with money try to keep news of the sale under their hat. And people will still find out where the former owner is and how to get in touch. Politely decline most loan requested. A word of caution regarding friends and relatives: When they come knocking on the door for loans or advances, in almost all cases, pass it up.

The results were disastrous at a very high percentage of cases that I have witnessed. With these types of loans, friends and relatives typically pay you back, last of all. A family member is easier to borrow from. And such dealings are much onerous if the loan or advance goes unpaid. Watch for these types of loan requests and politely decline them.

Professional consultants also play a part before and after the sale. A good CPA and tax attorney are great assets. But there often comes a point when you must take their advice with a grain of salt. I have witnessed firsthand a number of business owners who are somehow working for their CPA and attorney.

This is ironic as the said professionals should be working for the business instead! Most of these people know less than you do about investing. They have never met payroll at companies, leveraged assets or invested amounts of capital to get a return. I cannot count how often I have heard these words, "My advisor is against it." Why did he advise against it? Lack of knowledge or lack of understanding could be the reason. I do not mean to suggest that having a working team is not important. But you do need to keep your advisors and their advice in perspective. They can be a tremendous help when it comes to details. Your job, however, is the big picture.

Keep it in focus at all times. As a former business owner you need to give yourself more credit. You are better at knowing and feeling what is right for you than anyone else.

Carl was in the food business in the Southwest in the early 1980's. He served the company and his advisor told him of the need to own tax sheltered investments. He said, it was imperative to own these investments and Carl bought it all the way.

The 1986 Tax Act came along and tax write-offs were no more. Ten years later he was still struggling to produce cash flow. Had Carl not listened to his advisor his life would be totally different today. Business owners are some of my best consultants.

This may surprise you, but business owners are some of my consultants, and I am in the consulting business. In the last 30+ years, I have met and listened to more than 2,000 business owners. When I need business advice or help these individuals are my greatest assets.

They have seen almost every situation from being broke to taking incredible chances to stay afloat. Most business owners have wonderful people skills, compassion and understanding. They have had to be both tough and tender at times. Their knowledge can be encyclopedic.

If the former business owner has a close relationship with his wife, she also can help immeasurably. She is the one person who knows him better than anyone else. His well-being and positive outcome are upper most in her mind. She almost certainly paid a price for that success as well. If he does not have a good relationship with his wife, then surely has a confidant.

To sum up, business owners need to remember their own great traits. These characteristics are what got them to a level of unique financial success. They are their own best consultant. They are advised to select carefully their professional investment consultants and analyze all major recommendations in detail. Caution is the watch word. Greed and discretion and high risk are the cardinal sins of investing. These cardinal sins can quickly destroy a fortune that took decades to build.

Chapter 24
$15 Million and Broke

Most people would wonder how in the world a business owner could sell out and end up losing. Such loss can range from $5 million to $20 million! I admit, it sounds rather unlikely. Over the last 30+ years, however, I have seen a number of former business owners do just that.

They simply do not have much appreciation or respect for how much money it is. And, worse, on how hard it was to make such a fortune. Owners who lose their post-sale money usually follow one of three patterns.

Pattern Number One: The former owner who does not appreciate how fast a lot of money can evaporate.

The first is the owner who sells the company, for example, at $10 million. $10 million, anyone can live on that! Taxes after the sale come to $2.5 million, leaving $7.5 million as principal.

The business owner then buys a new beach house with all the trimmings for $1.4 million. Then he remodels his current home for $500,000. What is left is $5.6 million.

Both children hit up Mom and Dad for $400,000 of the newfound wealth. The new business entrepreneur, former owner, invests $1.4 million in a new and totally unfamiliar business. We are now down to $3.4 million in liquid investment.

The former business owner also needs to take $400,000 per year out of principal to meet living expenses. By the end of year three, the total has shrunk to $2.2 million in liquid investment. The business in which he reinvested is not producing.

If he does not get an income stream, his liquid capital will be gone in five to six years. Of particular note here is the difference in first, second and third generation wealth. Malcolm Forbes used to say, shirt sleeves to shirt sleeves in three generations.

The first generation creates the business, while the second age group sells, and the third generation squanders it. I am just as impressed with the second generation business builder. They realize what mental hurdles must be overcome to dispose a business and then to maintain prosperity.

This is almost the same with the first generation entrepreneurs. The group wherein most of the risk lies is the third generation. These individuals did not build, operate or sell the business. Therefore, they tend to underappreciate what it takes to make money and keep it.

Pattern Number Two: The owner who becomes an unpaid vassal of the IRS.

The second type of business owner is the one who takes public stock for his company. Then he decides to use part of the proceeds from sale of stock to pay off incidental debt. And then invests the remaining balance with friends who show up with the deal of a lifetime.

After investing into a more risky and illiquid proposals, he confronts the April 15th tax deadline. The staggering capital gains tax on the sale of stock is dealt with. On top of it is the interest burden on the loan obtained with stock as collateral.

Over the course of time, the business deals go bad and little liquidity exists. The disastrous consequences are obvious. The fortune accumulated over many decades is squandered. The once prosperous business owner ignominiously becomes the unpaid vassal of the IRS. And all this is because he needs to liquidate the tax obligations, penalties and interest payments.

Pattern Number Three: The owner who must be in business, even the wrong one.

The third type of owner who sells is the has-to-be-in-business person. After selling, he is so lost and disoriented that jumping into another business is paramount in his thinking. He cannot stand the thought of not being the boss. Over the years, I have observed so many of these people getting into the wrong business.

Having to be in business seems more important than being in the right business. Wayne exchanged his portion of a partnership for stock in a publicly owned corporation. Although he was a successful partner, he received a substantial after-tax dollar amount for the sale of his shares.

He immediately bought another business and, after four years, I sadly bore witness to Wayne's total financial demise. My last correspondence with him was regarding an IRS tax lien letter. My principal theory about these types of people is that their post-sale mindset is the crucial variable.

Indeed, I have known a number of business owners who have sold their companies and ended up broke. Interestingly, most seem to be relaxed even after losing it all. In my opinion, these individuals never were comfortable with a lot of money.

They apparently had a hard time seeing themselves as rich. In fact, they spent so much time with their backs to the wall struggling with debt. As opposed to the fleeing fling with fortune, that struggle was a far more natural state of affairs. Their adrenaline flowed most strongly when the battle was the toughest.

They seemed to have the feeling that nothing, even life itself, should be easy. They had a surprisingly philosophical outlook on both winning and losing. The success attitude is much more important than most people think. It involves a mode of thinking that makes a person feel worthy of success. There is very little guilt or negative emotion, only the belief that they should be wealthy and successful.

Sometimes this positive mindset is summed up in the French expression, noblesse oblige. Not to be misunderstood, I have tremendous respect for business owners. Many of them establish or participate in a second or third business.

They do even better than in the first enterprise, or at least, operate profitable enterprises. Many of the sellers who lose all their money do better the second time. In fact, most of them do just fine. From my observation, only about five to 10% end up in the manner just mentioned.

Chapter 25
Dot-Com Bust

One of the most overblown examples of financial hyperbole arrived in the form of high-tech internet-world investing. Obviously, the financial demise from, 1999 till 2002, what had been internet juggernaut, was devastating to the markets. It probably was a major contributing factor to one of longest market declines since the post-Depression era.

When these public internet companies started buying other business organizations, my 20+-year partnership, had been contacting business owners. We had been assisting entrepreneurial business owners sell their companies in an effort to diversify.

My partners and I had much more experience in counseling conventional investment clients in developing diversified portfolios. More than once, we actually questioned whether we might be out of step with the times. This happened when confronted with the outrageous and bazaar prices that the internet companies were paying in premiums.

Common companies bought were high-tech start-ups with virtually no tangible assets. We found an answer when we interviewed the owners of the take-over targets of the public internet companies. The primary trust of our message to them was in the form of a fundamental question: Why would you not sell your stock at current market price for cash since you have no revenues?

At 30, you have the opportunity to establish for yourself and family a lifetime of personal financial security. The sky was the limit in the dot-com boom. With one or two rare exceptions, almost every owner or client concluded the interview summarily.

Categorically, they advised us that the dot-com boom was expanding beyond any range that we could even imagine. This early phase was a drop in the profit bucket which would soon overflow in the not-too-distant future. The reply seemed to carry a warranty in general about internet market prices.

In fact, most of these clients would append a gratuitous dismissal to us, which said in effect: "Why do we need your firm when we have created all this wealth without you?" One of our clients, located in California, underscored the reaction above. In early 2002, Susan received a huge fortune after the sale of a business she founded. She had been in operation a relatively short period of time before the sale. During our contact, she told us we were like her father who believed in obsolete criteria about, and among others:

- Market values;
- Earnings per share record,

- Book value,
- Price earnings multiples,
- Dividend histories, and,
- Ratio of market value of shares outstanding to gross sales revenues before taxes and deductions.

The implication was clear. We were investment advisor dinosaurs. She told us the investment game was very different now. She said that we had not comprehended or adjusted to the changes. Almost exactly two years later, Susan had lost all her wealth. This is the young lady who told us that we have become peddlers of investment malarkey.

Arriving for interview with John and Ann, they both felt like the telecom gods smiles at them favorably. In our planning with clients, we always attempt to be realistic in establishing investment goals. We try to have business owners understand and confront the many dangers in failing to diversify.

Thus, we highly discourage them from having a one-investment portfolio or business. This strategic approach was difficult to sell to clients for one obvious reason. Each time we would present a plan for liquidating their stock, it would soar on to higher levels in price.

Literally, before our session had even concluded. In the minds of John and Ann, their initial objective of $3 million had reached $30 million of unrealized paper value. Their mental gears had shifted to the new bracket of a $100 million target. Since the large, initial gains were viewed as virtually effortless.

The upward spiraling price continued for several months, until the bubble burst, reversing the price downward and rapidly. Two years later, John and Ann probably would have been fortunate to salvage a total of $2 million. Greed was rampant early in the new millennium.

This story, and many others like it, is indeed sad. But in the early months and years of the new millennium, the greed factor is rampant. It dominated investment decisions and clouded the vision of a client. As a result, they failed to seize the opportunity for a lifetime financial security and concomitant personal freedom.

The mistakes were compounded by distain of the historical invcstment past by hubris. It was made worse by misplaced egotistical confidence in forecasting future movement of stock prices. Greed has other interesting emotional facets. The people who will pay the often heavy penalties tend to look back in retrospect and ask themselves:

• Why did I do that?

• What was I thinking?

• How could have botched this golden opportunity for financial security?

Warren, an Arizona client whom we visited, was enjoying the apex of the market. This was after he sold his shares in his firm to an acquiring company. At that time, his exchanged stock was selling at $70 per share. We suggested that he start liquidating the new shares, with no balance sheet value or other financial elements.

We also suggested that he include in his liquidation earnings outlook to justify the lofty price. In a typical response, he said, "This stock looks as if it is going higher to me." Two years later, the price was $5 a share. We never heard again from Warren. We also have no idea of what price he may have saved a fraction of his fortune.

Murray, a business owner in Houston, sold his shares in exchange for shares of another firm at $4 a share. We worked out a plan for him to liquidate these shares and begin a diversification program. Murray took no action whatsoever. At least not until the price fell to a minuscule 6 cents per share.

Entrepreneurial Acumen, Not the Same as Investment Wisdom

One thing I observed, during this boom-and-bust era, was the ignorance of the investment world among business entrepreneurs. Their ignorance was usually compounded with a dash of egotism and arrogance. They seem to have forgotten that a little knowledge is a dangerous thing.

They thought their business acumen was the linchpin of their newly acquired wealth. Financial luck and rare opportunities come calling only once or twice in a lifetime. In the history of our partnership, we had never witnessed so many benighted souls who did not realize this.

So many people, especially in their 30s, blew the opportunity for financial security and let it slip away. Their rationale is: "I know this stock will come back. It is just a matter of patience and a little time." I was asked by clients repeatedly in the 1999 to 2000 era to give them my best investment idea.

My advice to the 30-something people in the dot-com craze was usually to sell. They had never experienced:

- A prolonged market decline,
- A double-digit inflation period,
- A depressed real estate market,
- Trouble finding a job, or,
- Have other difficult, personal problems.

Most were doomed to hit the wall at some point. Only then will they learn how hard it is to acquire substantial net worth and retain it. In conclusion, we agree that high-tech revolutions will have the potential to change the world in terms of:

- Productivity,
- Lower costs, and,
- Speeding the process of vital data.

But companies must still provide valuable products and services, as well as, maintain profitability. Too often this reality remains in the business background, obscured by the fog of the fleeting euphoria.

Chapter 26
Real Estate: It Can't Go Down, Can It?

Real estate has always been a staple in the investment portfolio of business owners after selling. It has come in many different packages and most former owners like real estate investments. Because they had a business that owned real estate, so they, in fact, were owners or operators.

In most cases, they made money on this real estate because they owned a long time. Secondly, they controlled the outcome and, therein, lies part of the problem. They get the idea that all real estate can have similar out comes. In addition, these former owners have usually invested in similar properties along the way with very good results.

I too have been a (mostly) successful real estate investor. We owned ocean front properties that went down. We owned fully rented professional office buildings that sold for a loss. Go figure.

And there were several professional office buildings that went up, too. Overall, it was a net positive to our net worth. In fact, the last time I was the landlord was for a 90,000 square foot older building. It was a maintenance headache. But it was rented. The income can be very attractive. The tenant risk can be unattractive. Timing is slow. It is an illiquid investment. Financing can be annoying.

Most business owners, who sold their companies from 1990 to 2008, caught the real estate market just right. Declining interest rates, coupled with ideal supply and demand demographics, made for great returns.

Never-ending Price Rise in Real Estate

One of the trends we noticed, starting in 2000 to 2002, was a seemingly never-ending price rise in real estate. Practically everyone who sold a business also would purchase, at least, some real estate with the proceeds. The 15-year span between 1990 and 2005 was the perfect setup for the Baby Boomer generation.

Bernard was a former owner of an equipment company that sold out in the late 1990s. He and his wife called me one day in 2005 to discuss a waterfront lot they had purchased for $600,000. They were going to build on the land. But prices had gone so high they were offered almost $5 million just for the land.

They asked my advice and the answer came easily: Sell the profit and pocket the proceeds. The real estate craze was so big that they decided to keep the property and started building. A few terrible storms and a lousy builder, the profits were gone.

They ended up taking $5 million less. When the economy collapsed in 2008 we saw real estate at all levels decline dramatically. It may be a number of years before it comes back in price.

Investing in Those with Nothing to Lose

The other big mistake we see with business owners is investing in multiple projects with developers. Developers do not have anything to lose in the deal. Alvin was a client for more than 15 years and, during that time, we liquidated investments.

This was to meet the needs of his partners to build shopping centers. He could have produced a life time of income but chose to go with illiquid real estate. Today, we have no investments for him and his real estate is still leveraged. What he made during the late 1990s in real estate has evaporated and there is no liquidity.

The developer had nothing to lose and so it went from there. Most of his cash reserves up in smoke. Trusting all your assets from selling your business to someone else is risky business. If you must invest in real estate, then control the deal yourself. Do it just like you did when you own the company.

Seismic Impact of Internet Shopping

Starting about 2007, a new trend, internet shopping, emerged that surely impacting commercial real estate. This phenomenon is changing the face of merchandising. I believe that the trend will increasingly affect shopping malls, shopping outlets and shopping centers.

We often see at least 10% of empty store fronts across the country now. Internet shopping is touching almost every facet of retail sales. But the biggest impact comes from buying items and having them shipped directly to the home or business.

Offices or business spaces, which once were at a premium, are more expendable. And that puts pressure on commercial real estate. Also keep in mind that population growth rates in the United States have been falling for 15 years. Baby Boomers are the first generation to be larger than the generation of their parents.

They are also larger than the upcoming Generation Y. Baby Boomers have 78 million people, while the generation of their parents has had 40 million people. The next generation, also known as Generation Y, has approximately 41 million people.

Real Estate under Pressure

Lack of savings and retirement income puts most Boomers in a downsizing mode. This means that real estate, in particular residential and small commercial, will be under pressure. If you combine Boomers and their parents, totaling 118M people, then try having both of them sell property to 41M people.

Those numbers will be hard to match up. In addition, the trend among Generation Y individuals seems to center on enjoying experiences, more than material things. Business owners in the future will need to be wary of getting trapped in in liquidity.

In the past 15 years, the price has always bailed them out, regardless of the cash flow. Illiquidity can be the curse for business owners after selling out. They need the liquidity to produce cash flow. But they are locked into a maintenance-type, tax-eating investment with little or no net-free cash flow.

This, of course, is almost the worst of all words after selling. In many ways, they would have been better off to keep a cash-flow business. A disciplined approach to investing in real estate will never be more important than when investing sale proceeds.

From Red Hot to Ice Cold

Art was a client who sold a business in Colorado in 2002. Having watched stocks get hammered, he made the decision to develop land in real estate. The real estate markets were red hot in 2005, and he called, and liquidated almost everything.

The proceeds went entirely into real estate. By 2009, he had lost virtually all of it, with no cash flow and major cash calls. Such situations do not need to happen when former owners step back and look at the larger landscape. Give the same circumstances when they ran a business, this would not have happened.

After selling, business owners need to be careful about what we call the rose-colored-glasses syndrome – everything looks possible now. And they tend to completely over-assess their ability to invest.

Assess Real Estate Very Carefully

The attractiveness of real estate will also be there. But the need to assess correctly will also be there. Keep these significant points in mind: Be careful when your real estate investment cash flow is less than 20% of a high-grade bond portfolio.

If you are going to be completely illiquid, dependent solely on a sale or take out, be careful. If you are going to be having a partner, be careful. Very few business owners would ever have a partner in their business. So, why do it so easily in real estate?

Real property should usually be the cornerstone of the investment process. But the future will probably be harder than the past. Do ponder on this point.

Chapter 27
The Wall Street Shuffle

Most business owners after selling their company have proceeds that eventually have to be reinvested. That reinvestment can come in the form of real estate, commodities, businesses, or financial investments. In my 30+ years of investment management, working alongside people with 45+-year experience, one conclusion stands out.

The greatest risk to financial health and well-being comes directly from Wall Street and the firms they control. The greed that is spewed forth from these investment marketing firms leaves no other industry a close second. And it reverberates from the top down.

Watching people sell businesses, we have been amazed at the lack of skill, integrity and respect. This is in reference for large sums of money most Wall Street firm exhibit. In this chapter, it is my hope that you will get some insight into why this happens.

Several misconceptions come to mind. I will focus on three:

Misconception number one: **This one looks great**.

Firms have a tendency to recommend exposure, potentially volatile and most importantly illiquid investments. This is because they normally get paid more to offer these items. How many times does the former owner get offered a really conservative investment at a really low cost?

Many of the incentives for Wall Street are based on volume and quantity instead of quality. The former owner would never invested funds with inexperienced people, but readily do so, with newfound wealth. A shockingly high percentage of so-called financial advisors have little or no personal net worth. An oxymoron if one cares to look openly at it.

Misconception number two: **The wine last year is best.**

Money management businesses have a pronounced tendency to offer the former business owner investments that have performed well. This is normally based over the most recent three or five year period. Unfortunately, this is usually the worst time to begin investing in these areas.

Studies showed that worst performing assets over the last five years become the best for the year ahead. One of the reasons for this is: You will be the third party removed from the true money managers. Financial advisors, planners, account executives, and investment teams are people who do not actually make the investment decisions. Former business owners have experience in their businesses. And they often take for granted, the people they are dealing with, are the decision makers.

Misconception number three: **Former business owners are knowledgeable investors.**

When individuals sell their businesses, and have liquid funds to invest, they are usually underprepared to make decisions. More than 30 years of listening to business owners taught me a few things. In reality, most know very little or just enough to be dangerous.

They make assumptions in their investments they never would have made in their own business. When it comes to actual analysis of individual investments, owners have very little skill but rarely admit it. Unfortunately, many of the people offering these investments and advice about them have little skill as well.

The disadvantage comes from a total inability to decipher the good from the bad, separating wheat from chaff. Former owners are then relegated to accepting what they are being told. Largely put, wealth is hard to come by and, people who have it, need to dig deeper.

Just because you like someone does not mean this person is competent. Many former business owners know just enough Wall Street jargon and investment speak to sound knowledgeable. In the real world, however, they know very little about the actual investment.

Eric would continually ask me about the shop ratio, R^2 and standard deviation. He was relentless in this pursuit of knowledge and information. In 1999, he moved to another money manager because he thought we were too conservative and unsophisticated.

He eventually became sophisticated. Eric was less wealthy in the throes of the great 2000 to 2002 meltdown in the markets. Failure to understand how little knowledge the former business owner may have in financial analysis could be costly.

Following are just two pitfalls to be aware of:

Pitfall number one: **Too many high risk, high reward investments**

Wall Street loves to offer what former business owners thrive on the most: the sweet sound of high returns and above average profits. Remember the siren song of Greek mythology almost causing Odysseus to crash his craft on the rocks. This high returns and strong profits is what the business owner spent their entire lives trying to find.

They invariably underestimate the level of risk in these areas. Worst of all, the former business owners assume most of the risk. Witness the proliferation of hedge funds popping up like mushrooms on a damp night over the last 10 years.

Pitfall number two: **Over-allocation to the investment class**

Asset allocation became the ultimate buzzword on Wall Street the past decade. Wall Street took the concept to new heights, or depths, by allocating to almost every single area. When investors allocate sums of money to an inordinate amount of areas, they become so diversified. Being completely diversified means financial advisors do not have to make the choices on where to put emphasis.

Section Four
Clarity and Confidence and Comfort Begins

Chapter 28

Sudden Wealth Syndrome™

The United States of America is a rich nation. As disclosed in many research findings, the American wealth is extremely alive. The old wealth of steel metals, chemicals, and finance is substituted by new riches from telecommunications, computer software, and advanced technology.

Over $15 trillion of wealth will pass through inheritance in the next 20 years. This transfer will be from the Greatest Generation people to the Baby Boomers. Greatest Generation refers to people who have endured Depression and had fought the Second World War.

Incentive pay, in the form of stock options, is a prime factor in recruiting, retaining, and motivating employees. Consisting of top corporate executives down to brilliant young engineers, all gets the chance to benefit. When leading corporations are successful, these individuals may find their wealth grow into six or seven figures overnight.

This occurs when the option grants of employees vest or their companies go public. The defined-contribution revolution in retirement savings has created trillions of dollars in 401(k) and 403(b) savings. Upon retirement, many find themselves with the option of rolling over lump-sum distributions that can range into millions.

As the baby boomers begin to retire, rollover accounts are actually growing quicker than 401(k) plans. Rollover accounts are usually based on lump-sum distributions from retirement saving plans. To these worldly event can be added:

- game of chance winners,
- newly qualified thoracic surgeons,
- NBA rookies,
- life insurance beneficiaries,
- successful entrepreneurs, and
- Millions of Americans, all confronted with the problems, challenges, and opportunities of sudden wealth.

Coping With Sudden Wealth

New wealth can be of great benefit through:

- enhancing confidence;
- improving financial security;
- facilitating more meaningful career choices; and,
- the development of strong families and communities.

Unfortunately, these positive outcomes are not the long-term experience of most recipients of sudden wealth. What happens to sudden wealth? The simple and unfortunate answer is it usually goes away. Management experts of sudden wealth observe that the typical sudden fortune is dissipated in three to five years.

Pension consultants report that recipients of lump-sum distribution had spent every penny, on average, within seven years. During the 1990s, there was an explosion of new wealth, as the stock market soared. New wealth drove consumption in many areas, most conspicuously in new home construction.

But as wealth increased, debt increased faster, and the savings rate of the wealthy plunged. For the first time in 50 years, mortgage debt exceeded bank deposits and money-market fund balances. Bankruptcies almost doubled. The proportion of wealthy Americans increased by almost 50% with the overall percentage carrying dangerous debt levels.

This debt level is equal to the percentage among the poorest 25% of the population. Top 10% income earners comprise the wealthy Americans with a monthly debt payment equal to more than 30% of income. A larger proportion of new bankruptcies occur among the affluent than ever before.

If you are facing a sudden wealth increase, how can you avoid the mistakes that could dissipate it? This can happen to anyone through:

- Winning the lottery,
- Having my stock options vest,
- Receiving an inheritance,
- As the beneficiary of a life insurance policy, or,
- Retiring and receiving a lump-sum distribution.

We will outline 12 mistakes that the newly wealthy often make. We will then outline our suggested strategies for avoiding them. This will assure you that your new wealth will be a benefit for the rest of your life.

The Twelve Deadly Myths

MISTAKE MYTH 1

Making Impulsive Decisions

Sudden wealth is often overwhelming. The money typically arrives without the habits needed to protect it and manage it. Everyone you know is full of advice about what to buy and how to invest. Even those with no wealth at all would give advice on how to act like a rich person. Unsolicited advices would even include which charity to support.

Business and investment opportunities are offered. Loans or gifts are requested, or demanded. The entire experience can be terribly stressful, confusing, and difficult. It can also be exhilarating, like a big party, until the money begins to run out. Only then will regrets set in.

STRATEGY 1

Call a time out. Establish a "decision-free zone" for a specific time period, during which you will consider your options and seek advice. Then evaluate your emotional reactions to your new wealth. During this period, follow these rules:

• Keep your job.

• Keep your existing home.

• Keep in touch with your friends and relatives.

• Make no promises.

• Make no loans or gifts – to anyone.

• Make no investments until you have a written financial or investment plan.

"Experience is the name everyone gives for their mistakes."

Oscar Wilde

MISTAKE MYTH 2

Confusing wealth with status

It had been observed that most people who got their millions through their own effort have modest lifestyles. They also have been found to be spending little in comparison to their earnings. By contrast, most new wealth recipients spend above their means. They seem to believe that the material trappings of conspicuous consumption demonstrate their "wealth" and success.

Many Americans are victims of:

• Lifestyles of the Rich & Famous,

• Dallas, and,

• A thousand other powerful images from television and the movies.

These shows all equate wealth with material possessions, expenditures, and a lifestyle of conspicuous consumption. To keep our new wealth, we need to differentiate between wealth and status. Wealth is a lifelong abundance, characterized by a sustainable balance between expenditure and the income produced by capital.

Status, on the other hand, is the often transient display of material possessions -- the big house and new car. It also includes European vacations and designer clothes. The two values are always in tension. The choice of a higher-status lifestyle can compromise the real financial security of stable and sustainable wealth.

STRATEGY 2

If you want to stay rich as long as you live, choose wealth over status. Clarify your values and priorities. Make explicit and deliberate choices between competing priorities:

• Is it more important to live in a larger home, or retire at a younger age?

• To drive a newer and more luxurious car, or quit an unrewarding job?

• To fully fund the schooling of your children, or bring them on an expensive trip?

Your decisions should show your priorities.

MISTAKE MYTH 3

Buying a big, beautiful, expensive house

Comment: Nothing is associated more strongly with wealth and success than a large and lovely home. Yet nothing is more potentially dangerous to our long-term financial security than buying too much house. What constitutes "too much house" will obviously vary significantly from one person to another.

This common mistake is a variation of the prior mistake, confusing wealth with status. An expensive home consumes a great deal of capital for the initial purchase. It also drives a host of other higher costs:

- Upkeep,
- Furniture,
- Expensive cars, and
- Costly private schools.

The old concept of "Keeping Up with the Joneses" is not a joke. One of our clients, a bright guy with significant stock option wealth, works for a prominent technical corporation. Within a year after his options were bestowed, he bought a very expensive new house, somewhat against our advice.

Six months after moving into his new home, he commented that everything had cost much more than expected. The overall effect on his finances was significantly more negative than he predicted. His deduction: "Never gamble against the house."

STRATEGY 3

Wait for at least one year before buying a new house. Think of a house as an expense, not an asset, and only buy a house with liquidated funds. And may sure that, on this funds, you have already paid all taxes due.

MISTAKE MYTH 4

Spending nothing

Comment: Some individuals fall into the opposite trap. They spend nothing, feeling obliged to preserve every penny of a windfall. In some cases, they may even pay the taxes on:

- Their new capital with the earnings from their job,
- Witness their existence declining, and
- Come to bitterly resent the new wealth that they find only a burden, and not a resource.

STRATEGY 4

Establish an amount you will allow yourself to spend without guilt, and spend it. A figure of 5% of after-tax new wealth is a good place to start. Always require your wealth to "pay its own way." The taxes on your capital should be borne by your capital and minimized whenever possible.

MISTAKE MYTH 5

Failing to create a long-term plan

Comment: It is easy to enjoy all of the benefits of new wealth: a bigger home, newer cars, terrific vacations. Sadly, most fail in establishing long-term plans to sustain the new lifestyle for a lifetime.

STRATEGY 5

Work with an advisor who has experience with issues of sudden wealth, and establish a written financial plan. At a minimum, the plan should address cash flow needs, investment strategy, education funding, and retirement planning. A crucial component of the plan should be cash flow projections that address the questions: "In the worst economic and the market situations, how much can I spend each year? Shall I remain totally confident that I will never run out of money?"

MISTAKE MYTH 6

Keeping all your eggs in one basket

Comment: Often, significant wealth comes from ownership of one great company's stock, usually the company you labored for. It is enticing to endure to stay entirely invested in a single company's stock. This is with anticipating that recent superior performance will continue indefinitely. Owning many investments in your own industry is not real diversification.

The idea that you should have all your money in investments you are most knowledgeable and familiar with is not correct. You cannot possess the right, efficient and effective diversification if you only own what you like or comfortable and passionate with.

Advisors or investors will at times advise to put all investments in one place and watch them pretty closely. If all your investments were in, let us say, tech incubator Safeguard Scientific; at what point did you recognize that the stock was heading for zero? And when will you sell enough shares to secure your future?

No one understood technology better than Pete Musser of Safeguard Scientific. But he still lost a billion dollars by having all of his money in one high-tech basket. He watched it declining day by day, until a forced margin call took away most of his shares.

Enron employees saw their 401(k) values soar until the company collapsed. This reduced the stock price by more than 99%, and halved the value of their 401(k) plans. Everyone knows about "Dellionaires" or Microsoft millionaires, but nobody remembers the Pets.com millionaires. Probably it is because most of them are not millionaires anymore.

STRATEGY 6

Diversify. Especially, diversify away from your core holdings, and your industry. If your wealth is mostly in your tech company, your diversification strategy should be away from technology. These investments may consist of stocks or options. Do not own just technology, or pharmaceuticals, or finance, especially if you are employed in that industry.

Working with an experienced financial advisor, create a diversified, professionally-managed core portfolio to provide financial security threshold level. For example, an amount of capital sufficient will generate enough after-tax income to allow you to walk away. This means you never need to work again unless you choose to, doing work you love and excel.

Assured of financial security, you may confidently take risks with a concentrated, self-managed portfolio with your surplus dollars.

MISTAKE MYTH 7

Confusing capital with income

Comment: Without wealth, many individuals tend to adjust their spending to income, or combination of income and available credit. When the checking account is empty, that is an indication that it is time to stop cash outlays. When a large pool of capital suddenly appears, these habits do not change. Without the "no-more-money-in-the-checking-account" signal, it is hard to keep a rein on spending. To someone with an annual income of $50,000, a million dollars of capital seems an amount so large.

Our experience is that very large amounts of money can be spent shockingly quickly. Once a process of spending principal starts, it inevitably tends to accelerate. To make wealth last for a lifetime, new habits must be adopted, and effective strategies put in place.

It is crucial for the newly wealthy to understand the difference between income and capital. Understanding that a large amount is needed to reliably and permanently produce a modest lifetime income is important. It is very difficult to accumulate capital, and very easy to dissipate it.

What is a realistic long-term level of withdrawals from a portfolio? Depending on how invested, one million dollar assets might not generate $50,000 of annual income without being consumed. Stock investor, Peter Lynch, suggests that you can probably spend 5% of an all-stock portfolio each year - and never run out of money. Money manager, Charles Ellis, suggests the prudent number is much lower. His opinion is no more than 1% above the dividend yield of the stock market.

STRATEGY 7

Set realistic spending limits. Do retirement cash flow planning, using conservative (translation: pessimistic) assumptions about long-term investment returns. Remember, you must plan to increase your income each year to keep pace with inflation.

Structure your investment accounts to help create spending discipline. For example, only set up checking and credit card access to one account. Then transfer a specific amount of cash flow into that account each month. Do not quit your job, until you are certain your wealth will support you. Expected support should be the style to which you are, or wish to become accustomed, for a lifetime.

MISTAKE MYTH 8

Counting pre-tax, not after-tax wealth

Comment: This is especially important for anyone whose wealth is in an asset that is subject to tax. This means that tax need to be paid first as in the case of:

• Employees of companies with stock option wealth, either incentive stock options (ISOs) or non- qualified stock options (NQSOs);

• Retirees with lump-sum distributions; or,

• Beneficiaries of an inheritance where a large part of the assets are in retirement plans or tax-deferred insurance annuities.

STRATEGY 8

Understand the tax implications of your asset picture. Understand too the pre-tax amount of assets needed to realize a specific sum. This amount should be in values of after-tax capital that can be spent, given the liquidation tax costs. For incentive stock option holders, understand the two different clocks. These clocks need to expire before you get favorable long-term capital gains treatment.

Avoid disqualifying distributions. For non-qualified stock option holders, recognize that there is no attractive way to avoid paying tax. This happens upon each exercise at ordinary income rates. Exercise your stock options for only three reasons:

• Consumption,
• Diversification, or,
• Alterations in your occupation status.

In any case, only count your after-tax wealth. For example: an individual with non-qualified stock options on 10,000 shares of XYZ common stock. Such stocks vested today, with a strike price of $5 per share and the stock trading at $105. This has an apparent net worth of $1 million. This is a hypothetical illustration only. It is not intended to reflect the actual performance of any particular security.

Even when resulting stock is unsold, the in-the-money portion of the NQSO's value is immediately taxable upon exercise. Thus, a tax bill of up to $396,000 would be due upon sale. In other words, the apparent $1 million wealth figure is really only about $600,000. This tax figure assumes the maximum Federal income tax rate, but no state income tax. In high-tax states, like California, tax bill could be as high as almost 50% of the total profit.

Never exercise a non-qualified stock option without immediately selling the underlying shares. Keep in mind that up-front taxes are only part of the full tax picture. Taxes due on exercise of stock options are an example of up-front taxes. Prudent tax management strategies need to be part of your investment program for as long as you live.

MISTAKE MYTH 9

Giving away too much, too soon

Comment: A loan to a family member, friend, or associate should usually be treated as a gift. Generally observed, such amounts are unlikely to be ever paid back. Generosity to churches, charities, or political parties should be tempered by an enlightened sense of self-interest. Understanding of your own economic needs, both now and for the rest of your life, should also be done. From a portfolio perspective, gifts to family members or charities are simply expenditures.

STRATEGY 9

Do not make loans, period. You are not a bank. Defer making decisions about gifts, whether to family members, friends, or charity. Perform first your written long-term plans for spending, investing, and your mechanisms for keeping track of your progress.

MISTAKE MYTH 10

Unrealistic return expectations

Comment: During the great bull market of the 1980s and 1990s, common annual returns range from 15% to 20%. A study of investor expectations in mid-1999 found the median return expectation of under-40 investors was 27% annually. This, in reality is a wholly unrealistic number.

In the wake of the tech meltdown, many wealthy investors have lost faith in the stock market. They are searching desperately for new investment opportunities, where they can continue to earn the double-digit returns. And this is due to their need to sustain their costly lifestyles.

Today, the wealthy are turning in increasing numbers to hedge funds, venture capital, and private equity transactions. All of which claim to offer superior investment returns and the cachet of limiting access to well-connected investors. Observers from Vanguard founder John Bogle to Forbes magazine have recently warned about the perils of "alternative investments."

A perfect example of alternative investment is the hedge funds. Since late 1970s and early 1980s, an earlier generation of greedy folks fled the stock and bond markets. This occurred after a decade of:

- Disappointing returns,
- Placing their money in real estate partnerships,
- Oil and gas drilling programs,
- Commodities futures funds, and
- Tax shelters.

Like hedge funds and private equity, these investments advertised high profit potential and structural advantages over publicly-traded securities. Like hedge funds, these investments were risky, non-liquid, poorly regulated, and had very high cost structures. Many investors in the "alternative investments" of the early 1980s saw those "investments" decline to zero.

Richard Marston, a finance professor at the University of Pennsylvania's Wharton School, and leading consultant on investment strategy to pension funds and other organizations, lately noted: "In USA, one of our most prized ideals is skyward mobility. Unfortunately, in order to get upward mobility, you also need to have downward mobility – rich people have to get poorer. How do rich people get poor?" I dare say, through alternative investment!

STRATEGY 10

Keep your expectations realistic. Beware of over-optimistic projections, especially the temptation to extrapolate long-term returns from recent favorable trends. Know the long- term historical returns on each asset class, and be very skeptical about higher return claims.

Recognize the principle of reversion to the mean. This principle states: an unusually high return period might be followed by a period of unusually low returns. This was observed in the 1980s and the 1990s. Never invest more than 10% of your total investment portfolio in alternative (exotic, non-liquid) investments. Also, invest nothing in such vehicles unless your total net worth is more than $5 million.

MISTAKE MYTH 11

Not keeping score

Comment: "I cannot be out of cash. I still have active checking accounts in various pecuniary groups." The grueling tasks involve the sustaining, increasing, and multiplying liquid assets, not the spending of the money. The three classic ways to squander a lump sum are through excessive spending, poor investments, or misplaced generosity.

One of the best protections against exhausting your capital is reviewing your financial progress at scheduled intervals. You have to start correcting the problem when you realize your portfolio is:

- Declining in value, or
- Is not keeping pace with inflation, or
- That your investments are under-performing in the market.

One way to do this is to reduce spending or improve investment performance.

STRATEGY 11

Complete a written review of your investment portfolio each year. Track your investment net worth in nominal terms, and against inflation. Know the absolute and relative performance of each investment in your portfolio. Only count investments.

Do not include in the calculation the value of non-investment assets:

- Homes or houses,
- Cars,
- Art collection, or,
- Wine cellar.

All of these items are drains on your financial security, not contributors to it.

MISTAKE MYTH 12

Failing to get good advice, or refusing to pay for it

Comment: It is easy to believe that having more money makes you smarter. An example of this is to assume you are smarter than your parents. Do remember that it is from your parents that you just inherited a modest fortune. Being smarter also has nothing to do with you being younger, better educated, and watcher of CNBC.

Expertise in one field may be justly and generously rewarded. An example is stock options in a fast-growing technology company. Stock option wealth received as compensation for technical expertise does not imply expertise in a vastly different field. The field referred to is investment management.

In October 1999, Carl Russo, CEO of Cerent Corporation cited, "In the technology industry, astuteness is a given. The question is, how well are your smart people led, and how well do they execute?" There are thousands of very smart tech workers who were once rich, and who might have stayed that way.

Had they respected the intelligence, experience, and expertise of professional financial advisors, they would have remained rich. Unfortunately, most of them tried to run their own online portfolios. In many cases, they ended up losing everything in a variety of tech stock disasters.

Recognize that ability in one area does not imply expertise in another area. An example of this is expertise in computer software programming and investment management. A corollary of thinking more money makes you smarter is thinking you do not need other smart people. In his book, The Millionaire Next Door, Thomas Stanley notes the key characteristic of the self-made millionaire. And this is a commitment to getting, and paying for, the very best and available:

- Legal advice,
- Tax advice, and
- Investment advice.

STRATEGY 12

Hire smart advisers. To quote Ben Franklin: "Rent experience, don't buy it." Do not learn by making costly mistakes yourself, with your own money. Instead, obtain guidance from experts who have seen those mistakes before, and can help you to avoid them. Educate yourself. Your advisor should be willing to be a coach and planner.

The strategic plan: Employing a capable and reliable advisor

As wise old Ben pointed out years ago, it is better to "rent" experience. This is done by hiring an experienced advisor and taking advantage of his accumulated experience. More particular is the wisdom that comes from making costly mistakes. Do not "buy" experience by making costly or disastrous financial mistakes yourself. One can acquire technical knowledge from a variety of sources, but there is absolutely no substitute for experience.

In particular, knowledge comes from the experience of working with clients and managing money during both good and bad markets. A good advisor can put his knowhow, expertise, and training in the service of your long-term financial security.

Money can facilitate many positive and exciting life options. But few of us will have enough money to do everything we might conceivably want to do. This includes even those with millions in stock option or large inheritances. Make sure you understand what is most important in your life.

Furthermore, place your capital in service of your core values. A good advisor can help you clarify those values, and make powerful choices supporting your unique life plans. Financial Advisors offers several planning tools designed specifically to help individuals with large new infusions of wealth.

This may arise from stock options, newly-public stock, inheritance, retirement, insurance settlement, or other sudden event. A written Lifetime Wealth Plan™ or Investment Analysis & Review™ for each new client is always prepared. These helps translate values and goals into actions.

We measure your progress with a written Annual Progress Report™ each year. It is our goal to become your long-term partner, a trusted counselor in every financial decision you make.

"There are two ways to obtain experience. You can buy it, or you can rent it."

Benjamin Franklin

"Experience is the name everyone gives for their mistakes."

Oscar Wilde

Chapter 29
Comprehensive and Collaborative Planning for the Future

After selling a company, the business owner will have new semi-liquid assets. They usually take the form of cash, stock, notes or convertible bonds. In either case, the former owner has some investment planning to do. Over the years, I have met many recent sellers who had failed to generate a three-year plan.

In all cases, little consideration was given to the need for taxable income, inflation, safety or estate planning. The former business owner says, "I controlled my business and now I can control my assets." The investment world, however, may well allow him less control than his business did.

Questions for Reflection after the Sale

Our staff has always done a good job of creating plans for 36 to 60 months. All former owners are asked a number of questions about their future vision and their appetite for risks. Listed below are a few examples of questions we often ask business owners after their sale:

1. Can you be employed by someone else and be happy?
2. Do you plan a change in family status?
3. Will you be moving?
4. Have you made estate plans?
5. What has to happen over the next three years for you to feel good, both personally and financially?
6. Will you be donating gifts periodically to the children?
7. Will you start another business?
8. Where will your office be located?

In most cases, business owners have focused on their companies, not their personal investments. By asking some very direct questions, we can start to get down to the core:

- What makes this person happy?
- What is his purpose in life?
- Is he content? If not, why not?

Most business owners are usually working toward a goal or goals when the business is growing. They can usually recite sales goals, profit and loss information and numbers for the month. But when asked about their personal investments and plans for next year, answers are in short supply.

I often ask a question to business owners after their sale: What exactly did you earn year to year on your investments? I have yet to have a business owner give me a percentage return on his investments. Why? These individuals do not seem to realize that this is their new business: managing their money. It is still return on equity, but now, not in the business. It is still inventory turnover, but now, not in the business.

It is still gross margin, but now, not in the business. A plan will allow the former owner to think about cash flow, taxes, expenditures, pretax, and after tax. All this constitute factors in determining the big picture plan. How do things look two or three years down the road?

The next part of the plan is to look back after two or three years. This is to determine to what extent the goals have been achieved. Adjustments often need to be made or goals changed. In order to invest for the future, more effort is needed than just meeting and choosing among five investment people.

What are their asset types? Which assets are bulletproof? Detailed thinking and analysis are important to investment health. Most business owners are accustomed to paying themselves what they need while their business is private. After selling, a great deal of thought is required to determine the cash flow amount for living expenses. The risk factors associated with their investments need to be calculated due to the need for consistent returns.

Finally, consideration also must be given to forecasting the capital requirements needed to start a new business. That is, if so desired by the prior business owner. Unfortunately, these areas are often overlooked. They are much more important than most people realize.

Underestimating the value of planning is a classic mistake of former business owners. They tend to make nearly all of their decisions on a have to basis. The best approach is to have a nice flow of information and be prepared for all scenarios.

Chapter 30
Diversify

This chapter is addressed to owners who are selling their companies in exchange primarily for stock in the acquiring company. This is in contrast with other owners who demand a significant portion of the sales price in cash. The ladder remuneration usually provides a substantial gain. Also, it creates the first opportunity for the seller to develop a diversified portfolio of investments.

Diversification is a cardinal principle of most investment and brokerage firms. The entrepreneur seller faces a potential conflict of interest. His firm was the symbol of his business and professional success for many years. To own stock shares in the acquisition enterprise is participating in the growth of merged companies.

A business owner who agrees to sell his company for stock tends to receive a barrage of optimistic messages. The acquisition company shows recognition of his positive outlook for the current year and into the future. It usually emphasizes the contributions of the acquired company to future growth in revenues, after-tax earnings and finances.

This is a kind of trap. The former business owner usually believes that the new management has good insight into the future. Projected increase of per share price and earnings results from the growing relationship during the selling process.

These officials may have a special advantage in making prognostications, which might not be impartial and unbiased. The top management of the acquisition company is likely aware of financial and operational negatives on the horizon. These, however, may remain hidden under the corporate carpet.

Liquidate publicly traded stock of the acquisition company. I cannot emphasize enough the importance of its prompt liquidation. All, or at least most, of the publicly traded stock of the acquisition company should be liquidated. And it should be in exchange for the company of the seller at a reasonable price.

The greed factor for a few extra points is not worth the risk to wealth and financial security. Do not bet the family farm on the optimism of someone else. Then, start to promptly diversify with the accumulation of cash. There is nothing more fraught with danger than a so-called one investment portfolio.

The following illustrations will vividly demonstrate this scenario. Finally, there is another facet to diversifying which many investment advisors firmly endorse. Avoid the overweighting of investment selections in just two or three sectors of the economy, such as:

- Healthcare,
- Transportation,
- Financial services,
- Integrated oil,
- Gas and petrochemical companies,
- Merchandising and others.

With exceptions, it is not prudent to place more than 7.5% of total assets in any single investment. Many financial sad stories arise from the violation of some of these principles and precautions.

RJ, a successful business entrepreneur in Texas, sold his company in exchange for stock in the acquisition company. In addition, he received options to purchase 200,000 shares. In the summer of 1999, the price of the common share skyrocketed from $18 to $50.

I asked RJ if he was selling all of his stock position in the acquiring company. It was worth $20 million at the current market price as of the time of my asking. His options alone were worth the equivalent of $10 million. His response was typical of the complacency prevailing among entrepreneurs at the outset of high tech dot-com companies.

Although I can no longer quote him verbatim, I do remember his response. He stated unequivocally that the company had positives working in its favor as reflected in its price trend. I told RJ he could not be a loser provided he sold the stock. He had a 100% hedge in the appreciation of his $10 million …

Security is in the Mind

Everybody wants to feel financially secure. As a business owner, you kept building for that security. After selling, you probably thought your security had come to stay with cash in bank and no debt. Even the expenses of children are gone and no big obstacles at sight.

Life will now be easy because all problems have disappeared, but do this really happen? Only in the movies! I have two stories I'd like to share with your regarding security. As is my custom throughout the book, the names will again be changed to protect the innocent.

Feeling Secure with $1.3 Million

Gary was the owner of a Southeastern service enterprise that he sold to a public company. He received about $2 million of value and stock, and wisely sold enough to pay off all debt. He even placed $500,000 in the bank. He and his wife were quite frugal.

They wanted to be debt free with about $800,000 of stock before paying the tax obligation. So he lived on the income from the CDs and watched for potential business deals. I visited with them in 1987, 1988 and 1989 in order to discuss their financial situation. Gary and his wife felt very secure. He always reminded me that money cannot buy that feeling. He said he was perfectly happy playing golf in Florida then coming home to Tennessee to enjoy life. He was not worried about tomorrow.

Living for today was enjoyable and fulfilling for both of them. In the winter they would go to their hunting cabin and stay for a few months. They lived on very little money but they were quite secure psychologically and emotionally. The recession of 2001 and 2002 brought a big real estate bust to the Southeast.

Gary and his wife practically stole a house at 50% of value near a golf course in Tennessee. Biding their time was paying off. They, however, would have gladly stayed in the old house had this opportunity not arrived. They also had a chance to buy a glass company where both of them began working.

This started providing more income and then a new investment opportunity arrived. For $150,000 they were able to purchase 50% ownership of a car dealership. Each time I visited with them, they displayed the same peaceful security, even serenity. They thought $1.3 million was plenty and will be fine even if nothing worked out with the new ventures. My point is, although $1.3 million is not that much money to live on, it was for them. Indeed, security was all in their minds.

Feeling Insecure with $25 Million

My next story involves Tom, who sold a service company in Texas, and received $30 million in cash. He had personally experienced excellent growth in the company he sold. He expects to match those results in his own investing. Tom could not wait to start buying more companies and attain even larger net worth.

He simply felt that his net worth of $25 million was not enough to be secure. He invested very heavily in two banks, as well as, in three or four other businesses. This was 1979 or 1980, when most businesses in the Southwest were performing well.

Our discussions of investing in other areas were always too mundane for him. He could not see getting to his larger goals by investing in a traditional manner. He was very impatient with the slow process of getting there. At that time, U.S. Treasury Bonds were yielding more than 12% and the inflation rate was much higher.

It was almost as if he felt broke with $25 million net worth. Over the next six years, he managed to lose all the money in the banks. The same happened to most of the money in the businesses. The Southwester economy was bludgeoned during the early 1980's, as was his net worth.

I encountered Tom again in 1986. He was then trying to get a small company started with a new patent. His net worth was probably no more than $1 million liquid. To the best of my knowledge he never found security. As I have noted earlier, security is a state of mind. Everyone needs to be sensible with his assets through saving and investing. But there is a certain feeling that comes only from being comfortable within. What is security? What is enough? The answers to these questions are the exclusive domain of each individual.

In the long run, the key is mental security. We all live, we all die. But we can enjoy the comfort of financial security only with highly individualistic definitions. For many, the foundation of those definitions rest on frequently shifting sands.

Chapter 31
Enjoy the Ride

When all the checks and stock are exchanged and assets are transferred, you are back to square one. I hope that some of the information in this book has helped you decide which course is best. In any case, life goes on and changes occur. My personal observations about business owners who sell companies are, as follows.

Business owners are the greatest group of people to work with in the world. They understand risk, reward and achievement. Most all of them have had periods of high stress, serious setbacks and great excitement. They are generally an optimistic lot, invariably believing that the positive will prevail.

By and large, they are honest and endowed with high moral character. Of course, there are a few with negative character traits. Nevertheless, entrepreneurial business owners are the true builders of this great country's economic foundation.

They act as the twin pillars of political and personal freedom. Unfortunately, business people seldom get ample thanks for taking risk. Neither are they appreciated for putting their personal savings and credit ratings on the line. After they sell their companies, my wish for them is to have enduring mental and financial security.

When counsel and manage investments for former business owners, we constantly emphasize the idea of peace of mind. Life is short, enjoy the ride. What difference does it make if you sold for $4M and somebody else got $30M for his company?

As a business owner, he probably grew much bigger than he had expected. Even if he lives to be 100, life can seem short. Comparing or wanting to beat others at the money game leaves an empty feeling when all is done. Through my experiences of observing owners who sold their businesses, the truly happy ones had peace of mind.

In my opinion, success lies in knowing you did the best you could do with the resources available. A teacher who touches the lives of many children is just as successful as Sam Walton of Walmart. Who is to say that net worth is the only benchmark of a successful and well-lived life?

Over the last 30+ years, I have seen former owners render various kinds of personal services for others. One of my clients, also my friend in North Carolina, recently helped his maid and her church. He paid off the debt owed by the congregation where his maid belongs to. Another client in California lends a hand to many people he comes in contact with to assist them. To achieve their goals, he helps his secretary, maid, children, yard man, school friends, and just about anybody.

Jack was a fantastic businessman who sold his company then created foundations and charitable channels of all sorts. He was a tough guy to deal with but he had a generous heart as sugar is sweet. He contributed money to great causes and never looked for recognition.

The ability to help people was what Jack most enjoyed and gave his life the most meaning. My good friend and mentor, Frank Knapp, Jr, who helped me write this book, has always said that helping people, while you can still see them benefit in life, is much more rewarding, than bequests after death.

Most former owners of businesses practice this in some form or other. They give to people quietly without needing recognition or fanfare. In December of each year, my staff is inundated with directives by clients to transfer money to charities.

All of them are people who are giving back something they feel was given to them. Investing in others can be the most satisfying. Having net worth allows the person the ability to help other. And, thus, gain an even stronger sense of self-worth.

Many former business owners are helping people become the best they can be. The return on this investment, for the prior owner, is self-esteem and enduring satisfaction. The purpose in life of an individual comes more sharply into focus. This new world of liquidity offers the benefit to start new ventures.

This is done by investing in others to help them reach their potential. It must be done in a way that does not deprive the recipient of self-worth also. The people an individual invests in must feel they also are contributing to their own success. The impression should not just them receiving money from an outside investor.

Carefully thinking through the best ways of helping others is important. For the former business owner this almost becomes the next business. I have observed that most former business owners are spreading good deeds after selling. In the end, good work and helping people are the most lasting legacy.

Remember, the journey is just a ride a success is simply an ongoing part of that. Too many people get caught up in the wrong purposes in life only to realize this fact too late. Build the business, sell, start over, retire, there are many possibilities, but whatever you do, enjoy the ride.

Chapter 32
Tying It All Together

One thing all these stories have in common is the desire to make and keep money. Making money is the root of most innovation and achievement. You light your house without candles because Edison was in hot pursuit of money, not because he was in a state of bliss doing laboratory experiments. Adam Smith wrote, "there are only three things that make an economy go. First are open markets, willing buyer, willing seller. Second is division of labor, and third is pursuit of self interest."

Well the first thing one needs to do of course is to prepare and to plan. And whether you're preparing for your lawsuit settlement or your sale of your business or some other liquidity event, you should plan to optimize the tax effect, plan to minimize the risk, plan for proper distribution, income distribution of the funds, plan what your cash flow needs are, plan for risk management and plan for some kind of estate planning. The reason we do that is because we don't know whether we're going to be able to have our last check bounce.

Money maturity comes from decades of saving and prudent investing. Happiness is: wanting what you already have. Security is the freedom to pursue your goals. Success is the satisfaction of reaching your goals.

Wealth management includes financial planning, asset protection planning, investment management, tax optimization planning, income distribution planning, estate planning, cash flow planning and rich management planning, risk management.

Business owners tend to focus only on their asset, their one asset, their one investment, this illiquid, micro-cap, high-risk "stock" known as their business. And then they end not to be very well diversified.

Here's an "investment" example I like to use. In Florida it rains a lot. So I have an umbrella. If I put all of my savings and buy an umbrella, what do I do on a very sunny day? It's not going to protect me very well from getting sunburned. Or the other way around, since it's very sunny in Florida as well, if I use sunblock to protect me, it's not going to protect me from the rain.

So therefore I have to some of my money invested it in an umbrella, some of my money invested in sunblock. And that means that I've got some money not really generating value for me every day, because I'm prepared for the other side.

That, exactly, is diversification.

Now how many umbrellas do you need? Only one or two perhaps. One for the car, one for the office. And how much sunblock do you need? Well probably need just enough to supply to get you there.

That's asset allocation.

And it's helpful to face the investment reality. Many think that they are smarter than they truly are. Ask yourself this. Are you an above average driver? Most people say they are. And if that's the case, how can that possibly be an accurate statement.

Most of us have a "recency bias". We look at recent history. We become track record focused.

Most of us spend too much effort in retaining losses. Losses are involved with some cost. You can never retrieve the losses. You can help make up for them but you can't retrieve them. So often your first loss is your best loss. Some believe in some unfair advantage that someone has. There is no one with an unfair advantage unless it's not legal.

The reason we want to pay yourself first is because we live on income, not on assets. If you had all the income you need, why would you need any assets? Is that why we retire at age 65? Is it a coincidence that social security starts then? The entire concept of retirement has been spoon-fed to the American people by the government and many financial advisors for so long that few ever stop to ask.

Most financial advisors used to be called stock brokers. Most are better at accumulation than they are at distribution.

There is the access trap. This is another reason to pay yourself first. If you've got money in your qualified plans or an equity in your business, you can't access that money for variety of reasons. Why not have an ability to access your money at any time for any reason and tax free. We can show you how.

Part of the reason that people miss out on the best things of life is because they may hold some misconceptions, some falsehoods and truths. For example, you can catch a cold from wet hair or you pull one grey hair out and 10 more will show up. We trusted those who told us so we never really questioned it.

And, how many of us know someone who made a financial decision where the results have been unexpected or disappointing? Why is that? We are smart and sophisticated and try to make good decisions.

Couldn't it be that we made those decisions based on myth, misconception, missing information, misinformation, or in rare cases misleading information.

There are reasons why so many business owners, even successful business owners fail to reach their long-term goals.

And here's a dirty little secret. Most small businesses are not worth the trouble for most specialists unless there are 100 full time employees. Small business owners have generally can't get the benefits packages that they're looking for. So these business owners will not have a significant retirement plan or exit plan or succession plan. That's problem number one.

Number two is procrastination. It kind of catches up to you like a hungry lion. Early on in the business, you don't have any cash flow. Then as then business is continuing to grow, you use that cash flow to fund that growth. And because you're a small business owner, you're not really pursued that much. You must spend for yourself. So you have to depend upon the business income or sale of the business to be able to retire.

Three, to continue to grow the business it's hungry and it must be fed.

Four, small business owners usually started off with debt which eats into the margins and the cash flow.

Five, there is no time.

Six, qualified plans are expensive and a lot of the benefit goes to the employees.

And seven, qualified plans also can represent a liability.

Now why do I spend so much effort suggesting you pull cash out of your business? Because equity is like a balloon. Say you take a balloon and you fill it up with a breath of air. If you don't tie the balloon and you let it go, it might fly off your hand. If you take two breaths it might fly further. If you take three breaths it might fly even further. So the more you build up the equity, the more the balloon expands and then the further it can travel and the longer it can travel. Equity is very much like that potential energy of the balloon. Income is what comes out to make the balloon travel.

Conclusion

In the years of our company's professional service, we came across people with various questions and warning signs directly caused by instant wealth. Through the years, the number of people in this situation had increased considerably. More than a majority of these new-rich people though had succeeded remaining rich for their whole lifetime.

This is because of good ventures and company stock options invested in, as guided by a team of professionals. Those who got their wealth from inheritance had equally been successful. This was made possible by well-thought of exit plans made by their parents.

Financial systems and services handle the perils and prospects of the old and the new rich. The latter though encounter more problems being overwhelmed with their good fortune. The former, on the other hand, have a smoother sailing due to the preparation made and pecuniary expertise by their parents.

Sad to note, handling money can be a problem for those not accustomed to having them. Indeed, money is synonymous to responsibility. Thus, the more the money, the more is the responsibility. And as the pressure increase, so does the unhappiness and fear of failure.

So, attaining the dream of possessing much wealth is still not enough to make you happy? Ironically, it can be true and supports the philosophy that money cannot buy everything. What makes it worse is the emotional impact of having too much money or having instant wealth!

Without the assistance of financial experts, the people having instantaneous wealth can be plunge in a tremendous emotional turmoil. Feelings of false pride and confusion, coupled with a loss of purpose and direction may be experienced. In a worse scenario, it can break families, marriages and friendships.

So, we are calling out all those in such a sad state. This book aims to create awareness that there are people who understand what you are going through. And though it may seem bleak at your horizon, you are not a hopeless case. We are here to help you, if you allow us to.

There is no need to waste time on rationalizing and intellectualizing events and relationships. There is no need for you to feel:

- **Anxiety symptoms**
- **Panic attacks**
- **Constant pecuniary thoughts**

- **Depression**
- **Difficulties in sleeping**
- **Restless**
- **Pressured by responsibility**
- **Confused**
- **Loss of control**
- **Paranoid**
- **Empty**
- **Unhappy**

Helping people with instant wealth is done through coaching and confidential private advising. The methodology consists of acceptance of the situation, recoup on the distractions caused by sudden wealth, and achieve balance in life. Such situation, after all, is like finding one's self in one of life's crossroads.

At this point, change is unavoidable. It is your choice to make this change for the better, or the worse, of what you can be, and want to be. It is your choice to make the money work for you, or against you. You may opt to use the money to enable you to establish a heritage or squander it till it lasts.

As time goes on, there will be more and more people who will have sudden wealth. Some of them will be selling companies for one reason or another. They will either elect to retire, or to continue working with other ventures, a choice only they can make.

I hope some of the information in this book will benefit all those who read it. I am greatly indebted to many individuals who have helped me along the way. I want to express my heartfelt gratitude to all the business owners I have known and whose knowledge and wisdom have served as the roadmap for this book.

Paths to the future for business owners change after selling but I believe that the emotional paths are similar, no matter the circumstances. Life is indeed a journey and one hopes that after a business owner sells his company he can better understand this fact.

It is a journey made up of doing business, helping others, family and achievement. Nothing is more exciting than to watch a business owner achieve success after selling the company. In sharp contrast, it is also true that nothing is sadder than to see a business owner lost after selling.

There is more to life than the company. The owners who realize this go onto the next plateau in life with relative ease. The others never seem to realize that the trip was meant to be enjoyed for what it was: a journey that entails more than the mere trappings of prosperity.

Making a Living versus Making a Life

I am reminded of the insightful words of a woman named Sandra Kerry. She said, "Never mistake knowledge for wisdom. One helps you make a living, the other helps you make a life." Many thanks go out to those who helped me make a life in this endeavor and all the many business owners I have known and from whom I have learned so much.

Should you find yourself, or someone you know, in a position to receive the settlement, or to sell the company sometime in the future, I hope the information you obtained here will be helpful. Best wishes also to everyone who already has settled or sold. May you, and those whose lives you touch, enjoy the fruits of your capital, risk, pains, and labor.

Epilogue

Billy sold his business 15 years ago for $50 Million. He is a brilliant, well-educated businessman. Recently, he was forced to sell his mansion, and return to the workforce. His net worth had declined to "only" $12 Million.

How do you get a small fortune? Start with a large one.

While that is painful joke, in Billy's case it was a fact of life. Fortunately, he came to us just in time. We helped reduce his taxes, improve his asset protection, and maintain a reasonably high (though appreciably lower) lifestyle.

Billy now has a powerful portfolio that generates risk adjusted distributive returns above what he previously experienced. And it is very tax-advantageous. The portfolio is efficient, with little overlap, infrequent trading, low cost, and low turnover, leading to even lower taxation.

How? We put him in a combination of annuities, high cash value, low death benefit life insurance, and a multi-asset class global ETF investment portfolio with Dynamic Strategic Indexing™. We also created, collaborating with his accountant and his attorney, several Limited Liability Companies, and Family Limited Partnerships, and charitable entities.

He now lives on about $800,000 per year, most of it not taxable -- for the rest of his life. He will never run out of money. He will still leave a legacy. His investment asset base will grow. He will not have to worry about possible long-term care expenses. Oh, and he now only works because he wants to, not because he has to.

He is now quite thankful, living a great lifestyle, and worry-free.

Thank you to those who inspired me, and who came before me, and who helped me improve this book. Thank you for taking time to help the people who make this country great. Even, and especially if, that is you.

"Business is the business of America," according to President Calvin Coolidge. I am passionate about helping business owners. That is why I wrote this book.

We can improve the world, one business owner at a time. Together we can help more. Let me know your thoughts. Take care, and as always…Make great decisions.

Mitch Levin

Appendix:
CLIENT ADVANCED PLANNING SUCCESS STRATEGIES

Who and How we have helped:

Some of these advanced planning strategies may seem to good to be true. And yet, they are true. The names, locations, amounts, and businesses have been changed to protect privacy. They are actual advanced planning concepts through a collaborative and comprehensive process with accountants, and tax and estate attorneys. It requires a tremendous amount of work and diligence to be certain we precisely follow the laws and regulations. Not all can take advantage of these concepts. Not all advisors understand how to implement these concepts. Not all are willing to what you must to keep the clients "in the clear".

Coast Retailer—We implemented a "**Supercharged 401K**" including a "cash balance' overlay that led to income tax reduction of $1.27MM in 4 years, and over $2.39MM extra into tax deferred vehicle with over $100K to come out tax free, and the rest "stretched" over generations. The owner and his wife are putting in over $425,000 per year, with them receiving 91% of the proceeds for their benefit. Created buy/sell for his family to purchase installment sale of business while he retains control and the most income at long term capital gains rates instead of income tax rates saved another $68,400 per year for 20 years = $1.368MM

Sarasota marketing business **"Equity Rescue"** —Had $5.6MM equity in a building that was leased to their own family business. Business (with sales of $1.4Mm, salary/income of $130K to Generation 1, owner, age 70; business has real net pre-tax profits of $200K) to be sold to next generation, age 45. Children could not afford the purchase price. Installment sale of only 50% of net pre-tax profits reduced the pressure and the risk, while the building was refinanced through a new mortgage at $4MM. Business rent covered the mortgage and reduced the net taxable profit to each. Rent was applied to purchase price installment sale for G2. G1 gets $4MM tax-free. G1 owns life insurance on G2 for the mortgage amount. G2 owes the mortgage; upon mortgage fulfillment G2 owns the building outright. Including their additional savings of $500K in their 401(k) and $500K in a brokerage account, they now have $5MM on which to support their $130K life style over the next 30 years. Taking more than required minimum distributions (RMDs) from 401(k) over 5 years pays funds life insurance policy on G2. $2.5MM Fixed Indexed Annuity (FIA) nets $125,000 annually, most of it tax advantaged, for the rest of their lives. $3MM invested conservatively should net additional 5% growth for increased lifestyle or charitable gifting or legacy planning.

St. Pete—45 year old very high net pretax income of $3 million in a high risk, low value professional services business. Lives on $800,000. Has $7.5MM in cash only. Wants to retire in less than 7 years. Worried it cannot be done. Needs a risk transfer mechanism to protect against multiple business risks. We created holding company (**Captive Insurance Company or CIC**) to deduct up to $1.2MM in risk premium from the business that grows within the CIC tax deferred, and comes out at worst at long term capital gains rates, to the extent there are no claims on the CIC. Saves $520K/y in tax for 5 years or $2.6MM. Nets $7MM in the holding company, assuming a conservative 5% return on investments. Funding a permanent life insurance policy (PLI) at $575,000 for 7 years will yield him $450K/y tax-free from 61-85. Uses $1.5 Million for a FIA to net him an additional $225,000 per year, tax-advantaged from age 59 for rest of life. Brokerage account of $6 Million invested conservatively should yield 5% growth for next 7 years or $8.4MM in an after tax account. From 52-59 we must fund his lifestyle expenses of $800,000 for 7 years from the remaining $15.4MM accumulated (CIC plus brokerage) or 5.5% of that accumulated amount, after tax. Therefore we need to pull out 7% to cover the tax. Assuming a growth rate of 5% and 7% withdrawals, that is a net negative 2% for 7 years. Leaves him "only" $13.3MM. Then he gets $450K tax-free, plus $225,000 tax-advantaged or $675K/y, leaves another $200K/year to withdraw from the brokerage account or less than 2.2% of the principal amount.

Casselberry—62 year old owns $20 Million construction company with a fleet of 60 vehicles. Business has no profit, struggling even at that revenue run rate. Vehicles were leased at a cost of $300K/y. Lease factor only 4.2. "Imputed interest" over $130,000. Created and funded for 7 years **Private capital Reserve Strategy™ (PRCS)** to finance major capital expenditures (*cap-ex* in jargon) at $200,000 per year (1% of gross revenue, which we found by re-engineering the insurance premiums, and the retirement plans costs). That left him at year 7 with $1.6 Million (with tax-free interest) in the PRCS to purchase *for cash* the 60 vehicles. However, he did not need to deplete his $1.6MM. In fact it continued to earn tax-free interest at 3.2%. He used the PRCS as collateral and *liened* it with a non-recourse (meaning he does not personally guarantee the loan), non-structured loan against it. Non-structured means he can make the payments when he is able. If he had a bad quarter or bad year, and could not make payments, no harm no foul. He continued to make similar payments that he had been making to the leasing company. His $1.6 Million continued to accumulate tax-free interest no matter what. We structured his note on the vehicles to coincide with their effective life of 6 years. We recommended he pay the lien down at a slightly greater rate than commercially available as it only increased his *collateral capacity* for the next time he needed to finance capital expenditure (*cap ex*). So his payments were $243,000. A savings of $57,000 per year for 6 years or $342,000 total. Plus his $1.6 Million was now worth $1.93 Million. So what we turned a *$130,000 cost center* into a *$51,000 gain* per year plus a $57,000 cash flow improvement per year. At no risk. He now has the ability to retire on the *extra* $1.93 Million in his PRCS as well.

Minneapolis Printer--$8 Million business, two owners, with very low margins. $400,000 salaries to the owners, plus $300,000 profit. Each saves $100,000 after tax per year. Worried about returns on the savings. If they could get 10%, that would be $10,000. We restructured their 401(k), and their Property & Casualty insurance, and their mortgages, without staff reductions. Business savings of only 1% added $80,000/y to the bottom line. Now it feels as if they are making 90% return on their savings with no additional risk. This has increased their EBIDTA by 26%. Considering their industry carries multiples of 4x, increased their net worth by over $320,000. They are preparing to sell the business and should net out $1,500,000. **Process over product**.

Investor with **Phantom Income Tax** (PIT)— client of an accountant with $2 Million portfolio suffered loss of $143,000 in 2011. He understood. Markets go down. Unhappy with the $85,000 taxable gain as a result of selling more winners than losers. Thus had to pay $30,000 in tax for the insult of having lost money. Tax accountant sent him in. We fixed that using True Market™ Models. The multi-asset class global structured ETF portfolio managed to Active Strategic Indexing™, due to offsets will not show PIT.

This couple aged 60 owned a $5 Million business, "donated" to charities $13,000/y as a form of marketing. They were not charitably inclined. The tax-exempt organization introduced them to us. They had $1+Million in their IRA, intended for the benefit of their children. We found they also had substantial annual tax liability. We accelerated their IRA distributions (a **Roth Rollout™**, not a *rollover*). This required substantial charitable gifting to reduce the increased taxability. Through advanced collaborative comprehensive planning, including the charitable gift planning, we eliminated their current and future annual income tax liability from their IRA, and left them with 50% more after-tax money, while increasing their charitable donations to over $80,000. Good for all.

Hedge fund manager (HFM) – Very high net worth and income, yet in poor physical health. Recommended and implemented our "**Ultimate Gift**™." Contributed $10+ Million to a charitable entity controlled by HFM. Immediate personal income tax deduction and estate tax deduction. Purchased 10-year guaranteed annuity with that gift in the charitable entity, creating ~$1.1 Million income. Used that income to purchase high cash value, low death benefit permanent life insurance on his adult children. This created $44 Million of death benefit that is all in the charitable entity. The entity will gift away 4% of that annually or more than $1.7 Million annually, while the adult children can be compensated annually at $440,000 to run the charitable entity. Moreover, the cash value will exceed $12 Million in ten years, and $20 Million in 25 years, accessible to HFM or his designees, income tax free. To the extent HFM does access that cash value, he has further reduced his taxable estate. Charities win big. Current income taxes reduced dramatically. Children win big. Current and future estate taxes reduced.

NY Electrical Engineering Company Owner—Wanted to have income for life, principal protection, and purchasing power protection; he also was concerned about leaving a lump sum to his children. In a very low current income tax situation. Set up an **Intergenerational Guaranteed Income System**™, which works likes this: he deposits $5 Million into a deferred annuity which after 25 years will pay his children and grandchildren $600,000 per year for 55 years, enough for two generations to live on. We also funded a permanent life insurance policy and a high equity exposure investment portfolio. He will maintain lifestyle for the rest of his life, leave a legacy for his wife and children grandchildren and charity with built-in spendthrift provisions, have significant asset protection and maintain low tax risk.

Global Software Manufacturer—had most of his investments in solid gold ingots held in Swiss banks. Set up an asset protection plan using trusts, and multi-member, manager managed, limited liability companies. To strategically grow greater than the pace of inflation we developed an **Investment Policy Statement** that is evidence-based, and rules-based to achieve optimal risk adjusted liquid investments, through *institutional style* multi-asset class global ETFs that hold the worlds' great companies; and utilized high cash value, low death benefit life insurance as a component of the fixed income asset class because it has low correlations with both bonds, and stocks. He is now positioned for a downturn in the economy, his business, or an increase in taxation and regulation. And he can access more capital to expand his business, while preserving and protecting his financial fortress.

Child was victim of personal injury in PA—about to receive large settlement into his estate. This would have put him in the position of ineligibility for funding and rehab services previously available; and made child vulnerable to asset dwindling. Comprehensive and collaborative planning coordinated by us with the accountants and estate attorneys helped the lawsuit attorney make sure the child's settlement did not disqualify government sponsored benefits, and protected income as well assets for the child's entire life. A **Settlement Protection Plan™.** This included utilizing some of the settlement amount to purchase life insurance on both the grandparents and the parents so that future large lump sum deposits will see their way into the child's trust.

Divorcee aged 62 from high earning spouse. She did not trust her ex-husband's advisers. We helped her find new estate attorney, new CPA, new insurance agent. Planning helped her have a superior risk-adjusted investment portfolio to help fight future inflation, guaranteed income for life, with a doubling of her income up to five years for long-term care should she need it, tax free income to supplement, and helped her receive her social security payments in a lump sum, and tax-free, putting her in a superior tax position (since she was now as a single household subject to lower thresholds and higher brackets).

CEO of multi-state manufacturing company. **Restructured 401(k)** so that costs reduced by 1.3% of the $6 Million plan, netting out more than $78,000 savings per year for the participants (after our fees), increased the amounts the highly compensated employees could contribute to the retirement plan, without additional cost to the company, provided a more efficient, effective qualified default investment alternative to all the participants. Employee retention increased, tax reduction for the company, and productivity improved. Used the cost savings to develop the Private Capital Reserve Strategy™ to fund capital expenditures in a tax advantaged way.

Young business owner with $5 million in sales. New family with 2 children. Tax and liquidity are at issue. Wants to sell business. Particularly concerned about concentration of customer risk, interest rate risk, competition, regulation, limited pool of available opportunity, and access to capital. In addition to a more balanced and properly constructed, and tax- and cost-efficient strategic investment plan, we helped him by developing ***non-qualified private retirement planning*** using high cash value, low death benefit life insurance (PLI). Placed $100,000 per year for seven years into the PLI. In 30 years upon retirement, this will likely have grown at ~5%, un-taxed, and un-interrupted to around $20 Million. At that point, he will be able to *withdraw $1 Million tax-free, per year* for the rest of his and his wife's lives.

California low-tech business $35 Million in sales. $5 Million in profit. End of year tax bill was $2.3 Million. **Segregated** the business into Operating Company (Op-Co), Equipment Company (Eq-Co), Capital Expenditure Company (Cap-Co), Real Estate Company (RE-Co), and Investment Company (Invest-Co). In addition he established several children's trust, and a family limited partnership. These increased his asset protection, provided greater clarity of the true costs and profits of each, led to significant efficiencies and cost reductions (*after* the increase in accounting and legal fees, which totaled an additional annual expense of $50,000 or 1% of the profit) of over $175,000. In addition, the owner realized substantial net tax reductions of over $950,000 per year by using CICs to insure against his above mentioned business risks. After all legal, and accounting, and regulatory expenses, this will generate for him over $5 Million in net tax income savings in just a few years, and keeps all that money away from probate and the inheritance tax. The CIC then may provide the capital for his children or other successors to take over Op-Co and Equip-Co. RE-Co can sell with a leaseback, freeing up more capital for expansion. Invest-Co funded his charitable foundation. The legacy is a now a multiple of what the family thought.

Four-generation family office with $185 Million. Family dysfunctional due to substance abuse and excessive spending at all generations. Attorney/trustee brought us in to help to mitigate against the declining asset base that may dissipate completely after G-3. There was a $60 Million death benefit life insurance policy on the one remaining founding-generation member (age 90) with $45 Million cash value, and several $1.5 Million past due premium payments. The policy was at risk. We **stripped out the cash**, paid the past due premiums. Used the remaining cash to purchase policies on several of the G-2 and G-3 members that will fund an additional $200 Million for the benefit of the succeeding generations and charitable intents. In addition, the investments were expensive, complicated, heavily taxed, with much overlap, and significant long-term underperformance. Taking over the investments, using **True Market™ Models**, creates much greater efficiencies, less overlap, lower taxes, lower costs, while being more transparent. Now the trustee and the family knew what they invested in and why.

"In any moment of decision, the best thing you can do is the right thing, the next best thing is the wrong thing, and the worst thing you can do is nothing."

--Theodore Roosevelt

About Summit Wealth Partners

Summit Wealth Partners, Inc. is a fee-based, discretionary private wealth management practice with offices in Jacksonville, Naples, and Orlando, and with over $300 Million in assets under management, headquartered at Suite 105, 800 N. Magnolia Avenue, Orlando, Florida 32803. The managing director and partners of Summit Wealth have each been active in managing client portfolios for over 30 years.

Our CEO and Managing Director, and your author is Mitch Levin, the Financial Physician™ who may be reached through his email address: mlevin@mysummitwealth.com. For more information about Summit Wealth, please call us at (407) 429-6247 or (866) 977-2252, or visit www.MySummitWealth.com.

Please feel free, in complete confidence and privacy, to reach Summit Wealth Partners, Inc, for any shifts in:

- Your private circumstances, or
- Your business state of affairs, or
- Venture goals.

A copy of our latest formal disclosure record, in writing, is always ready for your consideration. Our firm is known for high level of service to clients.

Should you have friends you care for; who in your opinion may benefit from our assistance, please feel free to introduce them to us. We will be honored to be of assistance, in any possible way, to you, or to those who mean much to you.

Summit's mission is "to empower full financial health™". We do this through comprehensive and collaborative planning. We seek to help improve the world, one investor at a time.

It is our firm's desire to provide valuable, high integrity services to our clients. *Solid Growth. Safely Managed. Trusted Advice*™. That is all we deliver.

Thank you.

"I love the title and the topic. No one else is talking about the issues sellers face and how to overcome them."

--Nick Rodites, Business Strategist

"Unlike many that write on the subject of investing, Dr. Mitch knows from practical experience as a business owner, philanthropist, and wealth adviser. His insightful look into business ownership and how to build substantial wealth is a must read for every business owner"

--Ray Watson, Vistage Chair

"Great book. A wonderful job of myth-busting. I particularly enjoyed the chapter on small business owners. Nicely done."

--Brett Fadely, CEO Handex

ABOUT THE AUTHOR

Mitch Levin, MD, CWPP, CAPP, The Financial Physician™ graduated from Beloit College with a degree in English Literature in 1976. Afterwards, went to work in the Harvard Graduate School department of surgery computer labs under the Chief of Surgery, then attended SUNY Stony Brook School of Medicine, where he developed his interest in financial matters and was instrumental in setting up, what may be the first and completely student-financed long-term endowment campaign through insurance and derivative products.

In the early 2000s, Dr. Levin retired from active practice of medicine to devote himself to philanthropic endeavors and to his family. It was during this period, he became increasing interested in financial matters and investment Ultimately, this led him to begin a new career in the field of wealth management and he became "The Financial Physician™" and CEO of Summit Wealth partners, Inc.

Dr. Levin is certified in Wealth Preservation Planning and Asset Protection Planning and is an "AA" rated Florida State Representative of the Asset Protection Society. He is a two-time national best-selling author, trusted advisor and accomplished public speaker.

His published works include a multitude of professional articles and papers, as well as the books ***Power Principles for Success; Goal!, The Financial Physician's Ultimate Survival Guide for the Professional Athlete; Shift Happens; Smart Choices for Serious Money;*** and ***Cover Your Assets: How to Build, Protect and Maintain Your Own Financial Fortress***

You may contact Dr. Levin at mlevin@mysummitwealth.com

CPSIA information can be obtained at www.ICGtesting.com
Printed in the USA
LVOW07*0726060215

425978LV00001B/1/P

9 780990 790624